D1645054

WHERE THE BRIGHT
WATERS MEET

THE AUTHOR

WHERE THE BRIGHT WATERS MEET

By

HARRY PLUNKET GREENE

LONDON
CHRISTOPHERS
22 BERNERS STREET, W.1
CAPE TOWN : MELBOURNE : SYDNEY : WELLINGTON : TORONTO

First published 1924
Reprinted 1929
Revised and enlarged 1936
Reprinted 1946

PRINTED IN GREAT BRITAIN BY
LOWE AND BRYDONE PRINTERS LIMITED, LONDON, N.W.10

TO

W. F. WILKINSON

and in memory of

J. B. BLAIKIE

G. H. MAKINS

G. H. SAVAGE

S. J. SHARKEY

H. T. SHERINGHAM

AND

W. H. WYLD

" The Bourne rivulet."
(*Ordnance map of Hampshire*)

CONTENTS

LIST OF ILLUSTRATIONS

PREFACE TO THE THIRD EDITION

*I*T is twelve years since the *Bright Waters* first appeared, and of all the "happy family" with which it had to do only Wilkinson and I are left. Wyld, Savage, Sharkey, Makins, Blaikie, all are gone; and to their company I would add one more name—that of Hugh Sheringham, for though he never lived in the valley of the Bourne and was not bound to her by affection like us, it was he who made me promise to try and write her story. On one of his visits to the Long House he had found my fishing diary, and had given me my orders on the strength of it ; and when I asked him how he expected me to write a book about one little chalk stream, he said :

"Why not ? All your rivers and all your experiences would be to you but tributaries of the Bourne."

And what about the Bourne herself to-day ? Thirty years ago she seemed to be *in extremis* ; to-day she is on the high road to recovery. Little by little they have nursed her back to health. Even now she should be in danger, for drought has entered her house, and disease lies in wait at her door—the dread furunculosis is within a stone's-throw of her boundary. But her janitors have seen to it that no nether fish shall enter at the meeting of the waters. A grayling or two, as is their wont, dropped from the skies a year or two ago, but did not long outstay their welcome. Her family are showing clean and sturdy once again, her stream will run bank-high this year, and far down below in the chalk the floods have filled her reservoirs and bid her take no thought for the morrow.

I have made some minor alterations in the new volume, and have added a story or two. Be they old or new, all are but tributaries of the Bourne.

H. P. G.

INTRODUCTION

THE writer of fishing reminiscences is faced with three difficulties.

First, those reminiscences must be mainly about himself. Two are better company than one, and the true fisherman is almost as happy with a landing-net as with a rod, yet by force of circumstances he is generally alone, and, be he never so modest, there must be a deal of " ego " in his narrative ; next, the record must be mostly of successes rather than of failures, for failures pall upon the reader even more than on the author ; and, finally, he is cramped by the limitations of his vocabulary. A rod is a rod, a rise is a rise, and water is water, and no juggling with words can make them anything else. It is the dread of repetition which drives him to such florid substitutes as " the speckled beauty of the chalk stream " for the trout, or the " winged lure " for its enemy the dry-fly.

When we consider that the average layman looks upon the average fisherman as a monomaniac in magnifying glasses, whose motto is *Omne ignotum pro magnifico*, we should do well not to try his patience too far. If I tell him that on a certain occasion at Blagdon I was very much annoyed at having a 3¾-pound trout on the end of my line (a fact which I substantiate later), I should expect no worse a thing than his unbelief ; but if I describe that same trout as " the lusty Leviathan of the reservoir," I should hold him justified in throwing the book into the fire.

However, any lack of periphrasis is made up for by hyperbole, so the result may be the same in the end.

I lived at the village of Hurstbourne Priors, in Hampshire, from 1902 till 1912, and most of those years fished the Bourne, the little stream which runs south down the valley. During that time I kept a diary which chronicled the number of fish caught, the weight of each, the flies used, the direction of the wind, and other points of interest in the day. For convenience sake I used only a unit of $\frac{1}{4}$ lb. in recording weights, viz. if a fish weighed 1 lb. 10 oz. I entered him at $1\frac{1}{2}$ lbs., and if he weighed 1 lb. 11 oz. I put him down as $1\frac{3}{4}$ lbs., but as I always gave the preference to the lower figure in cases like the former, and as I never weighed my fish till I got home, when they had lost in weight, I erred on the right side, and my conscience is clear.

Though the book is nominally written in praise of the Bourne, and the social life of a little Hampshire village, it contains many other fishing experiences on other rivers and in other countries, and there are many digressions into other subjects. Such digressions should, as a matter of form, be collected into chapters of their own and treated as the privileged *obiter dicta* to which every writer of fishing reminiscences is entitled. But I have told the story of those ten years in its ordinary sequence with the thoughts and recollections suggested by my diary. I can only apologise for breaking the rules. All rivers and all my fishing experiences, ancient and modern, are to me but tributaries of the Bourne.

Any advice the book gives is, I needly hardly say, for the beginner.

My most grateful thanks are due to Mr. Merric

Bovill for the photographs of the Bourne, to Mr. Francis Giveen for the reproduction of the Kennet adventure facing page 176, to Mr. Arthur Rackham for the " Savage " Christmas card, and, last but not least, to Mr. N. W. Strobridge, of the Strobridge Lithographic Co., Cincinnati, for the "poster" referred to on page 6 which he kindly sent me and which is one of my treasured possessions.

H. P. G.

I

*W*HEN you travel from London to Salisbury by the L.S.W.R. (now the Southern Railway), you cross a high viaduct about three-quarters of the way between Basingstoke and Andover. If you happen to look out of the window on the left-hand side you will see two small streams, like little ribbons, running from under the viaduct down the valley and meeting at a bridge a few hundred yards below. A schoolboy could jump across either of them, and even in a wet season the water would not come up to your knees. They are mere brooklets, yet half-way down the first of these on August 29th, 1904, I got three fish, weighing respectively $3\frac{1}{4}$, $1\frac{3}{4}$ and $1\frac{1}{2}$ lbs. without ever moving from the one spot. This memory is not meant to celebrate my own prowess, but as a testimony to the little Hampshire Bourne, in those days unquestionably the finest small trout stream in England.

It rises generally—for its beginnings vary by miles according to the winter rainfall and its outbreak of springs—in St. Mary Bourne, about a mile above the viaduct, and flows into the Test two miles below. Only three miles in all, but those three miles the dry-fly fisherman's paradise! Except in the hatch-holes and the broad water below the park it could be waded anywhere in short waders; the water was crystal clear —the true chalk stream—and never got discoloured to any extent; it grew the right weed and the weed

was alive with shrimp ; there was, providentially, no
May fly, and the grayling—the grey squirrel of the
trout stream—had not yet put in an appearance ; it
was full of two- and three-pounders, often with
scarcely enough water to cover their backs, and it ran,
and runs, through one of the fairest valleys and one of
the prettiest villages in the South of England. Nothing
could stale its infinite variety. It had hatch-holes,
water-cress beds, broad waters, saw-mill shallows,
waterfalls and long stretches through meadows of
golden buttercups. It twisted and turned, it ran fast
and smooth, under trees and in the open, chaffing and
laughing itself into your very heart, for if ever there
was a happy river in this world it was the little Hampshire Bourne.

The Bourne trout was a perfect specimen of the
true Test fish. He was short and deep, with a diminutive head and a tremendous shoulder, bright silver
mostly, some yellow-gold, with strongly marked
spots, and looked a picture either in the water or on
the bank. He fought like a tiger, and he was, above all,
a gentleman. He was a devotee of the imago, and
seldom forgot himself so far as to pursue a nymph.
Bulging to him was bad form. In all the years I fished
for him I never used anything but the winged fly.
Nowadays the winged fly is looked upon as a back
number, like Beethoven, but I never put up a blue
upright, or a sherry spinner, without seeing in memory
the little winged iron-blue, sad, reproachful, bobbing
down to me under the trees in the meadow below the
Beehive bridge on the Whitchurch road.

The way I discovered it was as happy as the river
itself. In the summer of 1900 my friend the late Mr.
George Giddens, the actor, wrote to me to say that
he had rented the mill fishing at Whitchurch, in

Hampshire, but had just been called away to fulfil an engagement in America, and asked me if I would care to take it over from him.

We had fished together before under most delightful and amusing conditions. He and I and the late Mr. Comyns Carr and the late Mr. George Batten had once taken a beat of the Lea at Wheathampstead in Hertfordshire. It was full of huge trout and equally huge pike, and we had a most exciting time with the former with a May fly and with the latter with a gun. I shot about a dozen one hot day when they came up to sun themselves. We fished the pike also most successfully with an Alexandra, and, strange to say, the trout never touched it. We had a cottage just under the railway, and we all slept in a sort of dormitory— at least we tried to in vain until after the forcible eviction of Comyns Carr. He was probably the best *raconteur* of his day, and was even more eminent as a snorer. He would start telling us some story or other the moment we were in bed, and in the middle of it would go off into a profound sleep without a moment's warning and snore like a bassoon. He was the most delightful company, and the party was a jolly one. I can remember George Giddens and myself being woken up in the early hours of a June morning by cries of help from the river, and rushing out and finding Comyns Carr in his pyjamas and slippers playing a four-pounder and having forgotten his landing-net.

To return to my story, I took the Whitchurch mill fishing. I cannot remember much about it now except that it was a very small triangular beat, and that I got some very nice fish. We stayed at the White Hart and whenever the water wanted a rest we went off on walking expeditions.

B

One Sunday morning we determined that we would follow the Test down the valley and see what the country was like. The road ran round a deer park which lay on the high ground on our right, with the river some way below on our other side, and after following this for a couple of miles we came round a corner on top of a village and fell over head and ears in love with it on the spot. It lay facing us in a broad hollow at the foot of a steep hill. It was a gorgeous day without a breath of wind, and the smoke from the thatched cottages rose up in straight blue lines against the dark elms of the hill behind. The valley ran at right angles to the one we had come through, and in the middle of it lay the village in a golden sheet of buttercups, and through the buttercups under the beechwoods of the deer park there ran a little chalk stream clear as crystal and singing like a lark.

There was a church half hidden in the trees and the people were just coming out after service, and there was an indescribable feeling of peace over the whole scene. It was a typical picture of English country life which Constable might have painted or Gray have sung. We followed the stream up through the meadows past the church. We sat in the buttercups and watched the deer and the black sheep and the Highland cattle in the park above, and the wild duck on the broad water by our side, and we vowed that if ever we wanted to live in the country this would be the one and only village in the world for us.

In 1902, two years later, we found that our London home was too small to hold us. It is astonishing how the arrival of a small son can completely upset all arrangements and make two and two equal three. We had a charming old house in Kensington Square, full of panelled walls and powder cupboards, but when we came to look into it with the new vision no juggling with rooms could give us the nurseries and such things that suddenly became a necessity. We simply had to go, and as we had to go we thought we would give up London as a permanent home and try to get a house in the country with, if possible, fishing of some sort belonging to it.

The one and only advantage of being a public singer is that the work is sporadic. One has not got to be at an office at ten o'clock every morning. It has its disadvantages, too, as we have discovered since the arrival of the cinema, which has practically killed the whole concert system. The financial success or failure of the provincial concert, which used to be the public singer's stand-by, depends on the gallery. These cheaper seats held the balance between gain and loss, and at good concerts they were always full. But when the cinema appeared upon the scene this particular public found a new entertainment which was not only cheaper but permanent, and one which, relatively, made no demands upon their intelligence, and where, moreover, and above all, they could *smoke*. The house-removal, so to say, began at once.

I do not blame them. I should have moved myself. I blame the concert-givers for not realising that if they want to win back the deserters they have to offer them comfort and tobacco. The old-fashioned concert as a paying proposition is dead and buried, and yet the musical profession gets more crowded every day with candidates good and bad, trained and un-trained, fighting like starving dogs for scraps. It is pitiful to see and hear singers and players with great gifts performing degrading music to afternoon tea crowds in the hotels or in the limelight of the very cinemas which have ruined them.

The first cinema I ever saw was in New York, sometime in the '90s. It was a film of the famous fight between Corbett and Fitzsimmons, and, considering that it was the very early days of the cinematograph, it was astonishingly good. Corbett afterwards went upon the stage. I never saw him act, but I vividly remember his poster, which faced me on the walls of every town in the United States that I visited. All the crowned heads of the world, from the Emperor Franz Josef to Kaiser Wilhelm, together with the Presidents of all the republics, are grouped in a semi-circle facing the front. To the left of the picture Queen Victoria is seated on a chair, looking admiringly up at Corbett, who is standing in the middle shaking hands with Mr. Gladstone. What they all had to do with it, and how Mr. Gladstone, who probably never saw a fight in his life, came to be in that company, I have no idea, but as an example of pioneer work in propaganda advertising it was a masterpiece. But back to the Bourne. . . .

We hunted the papers for months in vain and despaired of getting what we wanted, when suddenly one day we saw an advertisement in *The Times*, saying that someone wished to let a small house at Hurstbourne Priors near Whitchurch in Hampshire, with a rod on a river close by. The name conveyed nothing to our minds. I got up next morning at cock-crow (I had to sing in London the same evening), caught the first train to Whitchurch, asked the way to Hurstbourne Priors, and walked along the same road we had walked that Sunday two years before—into the very village of our dreams !

I can still recall my feelings as it began to dawn upon me. It was one of the rare romantic moments in one's life when the fairies take a hand in the game.

I had not abandoned them with my childhood, and I suppose they had never forgotten it.

The house was exactly what we wanted, and I took it on the spot. It was then occupied by the late Captain W. H. Wyld, and I took over the remainder of his tenancy of both house and rod, renewing them afterwards on my own account, and there we lived for ten years. I wish with all my heart we were there still.

The social conditions of the life at Hurstbourne Priors were as nearly ideal as one could ever hope to find. The whole place, village, fishing and everything else, belonged to the late Lord Portsmouth, and all the inhabitants were either employed upon the estate or worked for the big tenant-farmer who lived at the foot of the hill. There were a few houses, our own included, which were let to the fishing tenants, so that it was like a big family party, and in less than no time we knew every man, woman and child in the place. I often go back there nowadays and just walk into the middle of the old life as though I were still one of them. Our house eventually became the best of them all, for not only did the landlord make all the improvements we asked for, but he built on a large addition which soon earned it the name of " The Long House," a name which has stuck to it ever since.

The fishing was run on the most delightful lines. Though the rods were tenants of the estate, it was in reality a little private club made up of the resident fishermen with one or two outsiders. There were no hard-and-fast rules, simply because rules were unnecessary, but it was agreed that fishing was limited to three days a week until August, during which month it was go as you please, and that the bag should not exceed four brace a day. This was fair enough in view of the size of the river. There were three miles of the Bourne and one mile of the Test, and, with the exception of a small bit of private water close to the junction of the two belonging to the Heronry, one could fish where one pleased on both banks and in all the carriers. It was also tacitly understood that, as there was no Sunday fishing, residents would not turn out on Saturdays more than they could help, so as to give a fair chance to those who could only come down at the end of the week. The season lasted four months, from May 1st to August 31st. This, too, was quite right, as far as duration was concerned, but I have always wished that the season began and ended a fortnight later, for the Bourne is a late river, and the fish are seldom in condition by the first of May, whereas in early September they are as near perfection as they could be, and that is saying a lot.

It had in those days a better and more consistent rise of fly than any river I have ever known. From the middle of June till the end of the season there was daily a steady rise of dun from ten till six, with a slack time from two till four, which meant that the whole of your day was full of sport and you were independent of the late rise. In the ten years that I was there I do not think I fished the evening rise a dozen times. The sport, like the little Bourne itself, was sunny—indeed, the sunnier it was the better was the fun.

The landlord, the late Lord Portsmouth, did everything for the water that he was asked to do, provided that there was agreement among the rods and that he was persuaded it was for the common good. Not only did he do this, but he kept up an excellent cricket ground in the park, where there was plenty of village cricket and where later we established the Hurstbourne C.C., of which more anon ; and he made a nine-hole

golf course in the open park above the Bourne valley,
one of the most beautiful spots in England, and,
though he did not play himself, threw it open to all
comers of all sorts from Whitchurch and Hurstbourne.
He got down one of the big professionals (J. H.
Taylor, I believe) to lay it out, and mowed the greens
and kept the course in order in the most sporting
way.

We were equally lucky in our neighbours. Sir
George Savage and Sir Seymour Sharkey lived in the
fishing cottage near the viaduct, and Sir George
Makins in the lodge in the park on the hill which
looked over the Test valley, all three famous in the
medical profession and equally good sportsmen—and
all three now, alas !, no more. In a cottage near by
lived two friends, companions in former days in
South Africa, W. F. Wilkinson, a mining engineer,
and the late W. F. Monypenny of the staff of *The Times*,
and editor of the Johannesburg *Star*, and very much
" wanted " by the Boers. On his return to England
Monypenny had been entrusted with the writing of
the *Life of Lord Beaconsfield*, and much of the work of
sorting the vast mass of papers left by that statesman
and of writing the book was done at Hurstbourne.
Monypenny was not allowed to finish the work, his
health failing before its completion, but the first two
volumes came from his pen. He died on November
23rd, 1912, " a life cut short in mid-career, rich in
performance, richer yet in promise." Presently there
reappeared Captain W. H. Wyld (commonly known
as " Poppy," whether from the colour of his hair or of
his early life I cannot say), equally renowned in the
army of his day as a rider and a cricketer. The call of
Hurstbourne had been too much for him, and back
he and his wife came and took the only remaining

house in the village. As everybody was full of high
spirits and endowed with a blessed sense of humour
the fishing season at Hurstbourne was a round of
rivalry and " rag " and practical joking. However, I
knew nothing of all this when I started in on my first
day's fishing on the Bourne on June 12th, 1902.

II

I EXPECT that every fisherman's feelings are the same when he starts on new water for the first time. There is the sense of adventure and discovery, tempered by the knowledge of ignorance. A trout-stream is not so bad in this respect as a salmon-river, for likely trout-water is likely to hold trout in normal circumstances ; whereas fishing unknown salmon-water without a ghillie is a sheer toss-up, for you may spend half the day hammering apparently beautiful pools which have never held a fish within the memory of man.

Nor is this the only problem of salmon-fishing. I have been faced many times on the Spey by an educational difficulty. Shall I learn the Spey cast or shall I try to kill salmon ? I have looked at the trees above my head and have always begun ambitiously on the lines of culture, but after an hour or two of ripping squares out of my clothes or offering large bits of my anatomy to the hungry waters (with occasional similar sacrifices from the ghillie) I recall the fact that time flies, and my holiday is short, and I relapse into the overhand cast and go for the salmon instead of mankind in general. The ghillie affair demands confession. I was fishing the Bridge pool of the Carron water belonging to the late Mr. James Grant of Elchies, and had just made what I felt to be a particularly fine overhand cast for the far side of the pool, when I was surprised to find that my line had never come on to the water at all. I knew there were no trees behind me in this particular spot, and I looked over my shoulder to see what on earth could be the matter. There was the ghillie caressing his cheek in a musing way, with half an inch of " Blue Charm " firmly embedded in his jaw ! He had forgotten that I was not fishing the Spey cast and had walked behind me. Providentially there was a famous doctor fishing the pool below us, and I took the unfortunate ghillie by the arm and tried to hurry him off for aid. But that was not his idea at all. He very slowly drew a pair of scissors out of his pocket and snipped the fly off the cast, close to his cheek, and then, even more slowly, produced the fly-box out of the bag and with extreme deliberation picked out another, felt its point, smoothed out its wings, held it out admiringly at arm's length, took the end of the cast out of his mouth and started to set me up the new fly before going to hospital ! Later in the week, as we were changing the fly at the end of a pool, he said :

" I hope it will get a fish this time."

" Why ? " said I. " Is it a good killer ? "

" Well," he said, with a twinkle in his eye, " it nearly killed me the last time."

If there had been a concert at Carron that evening I should have sung, " Scots Wha Hae."

I can remember my first day on the Bourne well. I had no knowledge of its possibilities or peculiarities. It was virgin soil so far as I was concerned. I did not start till three o'clock, and began at the broad water just above the house. There were plenty of rising fish and I covered them all right, but I never rose a thing. I tumbled very early to the fact that they were " cruisers " ; but even a cruiser runs his nose up against it sometimes, and I was much annoyed with them at the time for not playing the game. Later on I discovered that they were known as the "time-wasters," and deserved every word of it. What I chiefly remember of that day is that there were fish, real fish, everywhere, that they were "fine and far off" with a vengeance, that they were distinctly friendly—fish, like concert rooms, are either friendly, indifferent or sinister—and that any fish who lived in such a lovely stream in such a lovely valley would have been a blackguard if he had been anything else. In the end, however, I got four fish of $1\frac{1}{2}$, $1\frac{1}{4}$, $1\frac{1}{4}$ and 1 lb., and fell into the water pretty nearly up to my neck.

Between the 12th of June and the end of August I fished thirty-three days and got 124 fish, weighing $156\frac{1}{2}$ lbs. They were mostly orthodox in their ways, but the biggest one was rather amusing. He was a $2\frac{3}{4}$-pounder, and he lived in the splash below the Beehive bridge on the Whitchurch road, where the horses and cows and engines stop for a drink and to cool their feet. He probably knew every inhabitant of the village by name, and he had a profound contempt for me in view of the number of futile shots I had had at him. He was a beautiful fat shiny fish, and I never could make out how he managed to keep in such perfect condition, for his waking hours seemed to be entirely spent in chasing marauders off his beat. Either he was a night-feeder or had some private store of his own; I never saw him burrow for a shrimp or rise at a fly until the time when he made his one fatal mistake.

On this particular occasion he had gone down-stream in a fury at an engine, which had not only stopped on the bridge—a matter of indifference to him—but had sucked up water under his very nose, and then illegally chucked cinders on top of his head, and I had faded away with him down-stream with a conviction in my mind that I was somehow or other going to get him this time.

He had a regular routine whenever he was disturbed. I knew it by heart. He would drop down about twenty yards to a certain spot by the weeds under the far bank and, when the obstruction was removed, would gently swim up as though butter wouldn't melt in his mouth and dash suddenly into his old beat, scattering the interlopers like rabbits. True to habit he paused for a time down-stream, and then began to move up. He was in an awful temper. He had lost all his serenity and made no pretence of having just arrived from the country. He kept lashing his tail and making short darts at imaginary foes, as though he were bayoneting sacks or punching the ball, working his way gradually up to the splash. I knew that my only chance was to take him on the move, so just before he got there I put a ginger-quill in front of his nose and a little to his right. He turned on it and snapped at it in a fury. I am convinced that nothing was farther from his thoughts than food at that moment, and that he simply meant to " land one " on anything that came along. He certainly frightened the life out of me. He had been sacrosanct for so long and he was such a bully that I was almost afraid to take him out of the net when the time came. It took about ten minutes to land him, and when I got back to the splash there was another fish almost as big as himself already in his place.

This stretch below the Beehive bridge, and the meadow below, were then, and often since, the best beats on the river. They held royal fish in those days, and when the lean years came they alone came through with credit if not with glory. They are sheltered by trees on the east bank, and the water is full of weed, and the weed of shrimp, and the gravel shines like gold. It was in the upper part below the splash that a friend of mine, the late Mr. Richard Grosvenor, tried his prentice hand with a dry-fly for the first time. The stretch is only about eighty yards long, and the bank on the near side is rather high, so that you have to keep very low and throw a long line. He managed this part of it all right, and the hospitable Bourne trout responded with such splendid loyalty that before he knew where he was he was into three two-pounders in succession. He hooked and lost each one in the space of about five seconds, and all in the same way. He was so excited when he saw them go for the fly that he leapt to his feet, staggered down the bank and fell flat on his back. He did this three times running, and each time the fly and the point went to glory, and as he was using my rod I was thankful when that particular beat was exhausted.

I see that on the same day that I got the big one mentioned above I got three others of 2¼, 1½ and 1 lb. in these meadows, and another next morning of 2¼ lbs. When I think of the respect in which two-pounders are held in the deep heavy waters of the upper Kennet, and other great trout-rivers, I feel all the more admiration for the little Bourne.

This beat was remarkable in another way. The water was shallow and crystal clear, and the gravel patches acted almost as reflectors, so that you could see everything that the fish did and almost tell what they were thinking about. If you kept far enough off you could experiment with any one of them and watch the whole process. It was both instructive and amusing to see how one fish would be indifferent to the fly which

floated straight down over his head, but would at
once display interest, or even enthusiasm, about a dun
which came down a foot to his right ; another would
freeze from unconcern to suspicion the moment he
saw it, and turn, apparently, to marble ; another would
let it sail a foot past him without a sign, then suddenly
turn and follow it down-stream. It was often possible
by a simple process of elimination to discover the one
weak point in the defence of any individual enemy and
store it away in one's mind to be used on a later
occasion.

This stretch disposed for ever of the fallacy that
the tailing fish will not rise to a fly. I have caught
dozens of them in these two fields alone. It depends
upon two things, first whether you can see the whole
fish, his entire personality, not merely his tail wagging
about in the air as he burrows, and secondly the pace
and energy of his excavations. If he is really shrimp-
hungry, and keen on his job, and dashes his nose down
into the weed, exploring every inch in slow time as he
goes, you may give him up. But if he is sauntering up
the water, and lazily nosing into the weed at casual
intervals, you are as likely as not to get him ; indeed,
more likely than if he is rising regularly at fly, for his
active mind is so reposefully switched on to shrimp
that he subconsciously sucks in the passing fly without
thinking, and you are under his guard before he
has time to pull himself together. He is so lazily
absorbed in shrimping that you can take far greater
liberties in the matter of approach than if he were
rising. I have followed a tailing fish fifty yards up the
Test, and got him in the end, and I have known from
the beginning that I was going to get him if I kept
long enough at it. On the other hand, how many times
have I followed his like, casting over him and always

just going to get him, with the result that he has either come to the top of his beat and turned round and swum past me, incidentally getting the shock of his life at the ugly apparition on the bank, or he has dropped gently back, and I have dropped back with him and on to my back over a stump or a stone! I have never found the expedient of whacking a great big fly with a splash over a tailer's nose of the slightest use. He either takes no notice of it or bolts for cover. He certainly never takes it. It is the fisherman's sixth sense which tells you which tailer you can tackle and which is a "time-waster."

III

WILD LIFE IN THE BOURNE VALLEY (1903)

THE broad water of the Bourne begins below the iron bridge which carries the road to St. Mary Bourne. The water here rushes strongly through the arches, and there has always been a back eddy by the near arch, and that back eddy in those days always held a good fish. He lay at right angles to the stream in shallow water, and hugged the wall and watched the traffic on the road above out of the back of his head. It was possible to see him by crawling up to the bridge and putting one's eye round the corner like a fox-terrier waiting for the postman. It was also an easy cast from the road, but after trying that game once or twice to his intense amusement, I blushingly gave it up. I either had to get him from below or not at all. But here I was faced by the fact that, try as I would, I was invariably defeated by the drag. If I threw directly in front of him the back eddy swished the fly across his nose and drowned it, and if I threw in a bunch and trusted to luck the main stream whipped it out, and in either case he was off for the next half-hour. It was maddening to be beaten each time and to see a good fish flaunting himself in the open and treating me with contempt. It infuriated me, and I kept pegging away at him day after day ; and then all of a sudden, one afternoon, I saw my fly float, beautifully cocked, right up the channel over his nose and he took it at once.

This particular fish was a long ugly beast, as I knew, with a huge head and teeth like a dog, and better out of the water than in it, but that was not the point. The thing was that it was possible after all to do the apparently impossible and float a fly into that impenetrable dug-out, and that the laugh at last was on the other side. I remembered that on this particular occasion my fly had caught up on a patch of lichen growing on the bridge, and had taken an appreciable time to fall off. I had tried dozens of times the expedient of hitting the bridge first, but it had never come off till now. I knew that there would soon be another, and probably better, tenant of this lie, so I went back and experimented for half an hour, and found that nearly every time I hit that particular bit of lichen the fly behaved like a lady and sailed up the back eddy in a dignified manner.

It was a great discovery and got me several fine fish that season, until they, too, found it out and deserted the spot—for fish have some occult power of warning one another or extracting wisdom from the fate of their neighbours. I deal further with this later on.

The secret of this particular cast probably was that the momentary hesitation of the fly, when it was caught up in the lichen, gave the cast time to belly round the swirl and pull the point gently up the slack water.

I did not always have it my own way here, however, for the very next day I lost the new tenant and two others in the same pool, one owing to my reel jamming, another because the butt caught in my watch-chain, and the third because it leaped out of the water with a parabola like a rainbow and dazed me into practical insensibility.

C

I had an exciting time one day in July with a $2\frac{1}{2}$-pounder at the junction of the Bourne and the Test. They meet at right angles at the bottom of the Heronry garden, and rush at great speed through a hatch into a deep drop on the other side. I got into him in the Bourne about thirty yards above the hatch, and he ran up-stream with perfect good taste, but then he suddenly darted back, raced past me to the hatch, and was sucked through in a moment and thrown out into the stream about ten yards below, where he lay, still on the hook, swinging backwards and forwards in the current.

It was impossible to pass the rod through the hatch, and equally impossible to stick the spike into the ground, for this particular spot was either hard stones or soft mud, so I had to wade across and lash the rod firmly to a pollard. I then went down below the hatch and netted him there. It was not exactly orthodox, but any port in a storm! He was too bewildered by his experiences to give me any trouble, but it was less easy than it sounds, for the cows were in the water and he was washing about against their knees, and I had more trouble in shepherding them than in landing him! I had a far more complicated and exciting experience of the same sort once on the Kennet which I hope to tell later.

It was on this same day, and just above this spot, that I saw a stoat kill a wild duck, and I can remember now the blind fury with which I dashed across the river and tried to murder him—the pot calling the kettle black!

It is one of the most interesting things about fishing that one is admitted almost automatically to the intimate side of wild life. Moments such as I have described, when the blood-lust makes wild things

blind, are not the whole of it. Above and beyond
there seems to be a subtle recognition of the fact that
the fisherman is bent on other matters, and that he
may be looked upon either as a friend, which he certainly is, or as unconcerned and therefore not to be
shunned. It is a commonplace that if you walk
through a field of cows or horses with a rod over your
shoulder they will go on feeding unconcernedly,
whereas if you had an ordinary stick in your hand they
would make haste to get out of your way, and the
same thing seems to apply to the swallows and swifts
and bird-life generally.

General Cooper told me that shortly after the completion of the Uganda Railway in 1903, steps were
taken to prevent the indiscriminate slaughter of the
huge herds of antelope and big game in the country
through which the railway passed. As a matter of
convenience the track itself was taken as a boundary,
and one side of the line was made " out of bounds "
for shooting. For about 150 miles of this track the
line ran through open grazing country carrying
innumerable herds of antelope, hartebeeste, Grant's
gazelles, wildebeeste, giraffe, ostrich, etc.

For a while after the institution of the reserve the
game would scatter in all directions on the approach
of the train. After some time, however, they would
barely interrupt their grazing, and would merely look
curiously at the strange beast that apparently never
hurt them. After a further lapse of time the north side
of the track became almost deserted, whilst on the
south side (the reserve) they continued to play about
and feed close up to the line and in hardly diminished
numbers. The line itself is a single unfenced track,
but the game had learned that on one side was safety
and on the other peril. The topography and the

grazing were identical on each side. Sheringham told me that he had often seen the herons doing the same thing by the Fairford line. He once counted thirteen in one field.

The stoat is a puzzling creature. At one time he will run from you for his life, and at another he will take no notice of you whatever. I remember one which came out of the long grass by the Bourne and walked deliberately right across both my feet and into the grass beyond. He certainly was not on the kill, but he must have been thinking of something important. It was about the only time in my life that one of his sort did not inspire me with the wish to kill him for killing the things I love. He was so gentle and confiding that I let him go in peace.

I remember, too, standing beside a footbridge below the church at Hurstbourne and seeing a stoat emerge out of the flags at my feet with a dead water-rat in his mouth and carry it on to the plank in front of me. It was as big as he was, and he pushed it across the bridge in front of him, stopping every couple of feet to rest.

But I had one experience with a stoat which I shall never forget. I had been fishing close to Savage's cottage, and was coming down through the meadow to get to the lower water, when a hare came loping across the field, and sat down quite close to me and gazed up at me pathetically. I had not a notion what it all meant, for a hare does not generally seek man's company or move so deliberately into danger, and I came to the conclusion that it must be blind ; and then I became aware of a small object moving towards us from the far side of the meadow, and I realised that I was actually witnessing a thing of which I had often heard, and which I had never before seen—a stoat running a hare down. I had heard that if it once starts

BELOW THE VIADUCT (MERRIC BOVILL)

it will follow a hare all day across country until it wears it down. It came across to within fifteen yards of me, and sat up. The hare was sitting up almost at my feet, and there we stayed and looked at one another. Then I picked up a stone, the only weapon I could find, and threw it at the stoat, and never have I regretted so much that my hand had lost the cunning of my boyhood in Ireland, where stone-throwing is a fine art. I missed it, of course, and it made off in one direction and the hare in the other. It must have got the poor thing in the end, but I still can see that hare's appealing eyes and feel the shamefaced glow of pride that when it was in deadly peril it came to me for help.

The hare was not alone in that respect. In the summer of 1911, the year of the great heat, we practically lived in the hall of the Long House as the only cool spot in the place. We were at luncheon there one day when a swallow dashed in through the open door and swooped round our heads, calling at the top of his voice. We thought at first that he had come in by mistake and was frightened by his audience, but when he flew out and in again several times calling to us all the while we guessed that something was wrong and that he was asking us to come and help. I jumped up and ran outside. He flew backwards and forwards through the porch, telling me to look up. There was a strong Jackmannia creeper over the porch, kept in its place inside by a net, and in one of the meshes his mate was hanging by her neck. I had my knife out in a moment and cut her down. She seemed past help, poor little soul, but I laid her on the path and dropped water on her head—the only thing I could think of at the moment—while he flew round and round beseeching her by name. For a long, long time she lay there without a movement, then she stirred a little, and then she lifted her head and suddenly up she got and off they went together calling to high Heaven for joy.

In this context I am going to anticipate. On my return from Germany (to which I refer in the next chapter) my parents took an old house in Sussex for the spring and summer. There was a wonderful old barn in the farmyard, beautiful to look at but built on the cock-eyed principle of putting a roof of huge stone slabs on to walls of wooden planks. I was walking through the farmyard one morning and had just passed through the barn and was climbing the bank up to the meadow on the other side when there was a roaring crash behind me and there was the barn in ruins on the ground. Vast clouds of dust were rising into the air and I was standing there thanking my stars that it had deferred its end till I was out of the way, when I felt something give me a gentle shove in the middle of my back. I turned round and there behind me were a dozen cows with two horses in front of them, one of which had been chosen by the unwritten law as their ambassador to ask me what the something or other I had been and gone and done to their barn.

The degrees of mental superiority, silently acknowledged and obeyed, in domestic animals are most instructive. If you throw an armful of cut grass over the fence into a cowfield the cows will eat it tranquilly. But let a horse come along, and the cows will make him a humble obeisance and retire from the scene.

We are so accustomed to such animal snobbery that we take it for granted, but it was once vividly illustrated for my benefit. I was fishing a few summers ago on Lough Mask in Ireland, and one day, in the early hours of the morning, I was woken by a terrific noise outside my window. I leapt from my bed and looked out, and there below me was a stampede of cows, horses, donkeys, goats, turkeys, ducks and hens galloping for their lives—with a diminutive York-shire-cum-black-and-tan terrier yapping at their heels!

The Bourne fish, though a highly trained opponent to the old hand, was sometimes very kind to beginners. A nephew of mine at Eton (now familiar to readers of the *Field* as " Mugdrum ") came over for his long leave to Hurstbourne and got four very good fish and lost two others. He had never thrown a dry-fly in his life, and he was promptly inoculated with the disease, and has been a mad dry-fly man ever since. The same applied to another Eton boy, Merric Bovill, with whom I have often fished since. He learned his first dry-fly lesson that year on the Bourne, and blooded himself with a 2½ pounder in almost the exact place below the viaduct where I got the three I spoke of before. (The crime is reconstructed in the accom-panying photograph, which shows chiefly the futility of a man of thirty-five trying to look like a boy of sixteen.) He went to Norway that summer, where he promptly proceeded to kill forty salmon in a fortnight.

On the same day I got six fish weighing 9½ lbs., a very fair sample of what the Bourne was prepared to do for her friends.

In 1903 I fished fifty-one days and got 165 fish weighing 233¼ lbs. This works out at just under 1½ lbs. a fish, but in view of the rules I followed with regard to weighing, of which I spoke earlier, the average was really over, not under, this weight. I had no blank day, and I finished up with the biggest and best fish I ever caught in either Bourne or Test.

IV

THE FINEST TROUT IN THE RIVER

IT might naturally be supposed that if one had
the fishing of a trout-stream like the Bourne one
would not leave an inch of it unexplored, but it was a
fact that up to this time none of the rods had ever taken
the trouble to investigate the top quarter-mile of the
water. Savage and Sharkey had somehow got it into
their heads that there was nothing worth troubling
about above the " lagoon " immediately beyond the
viaduct, and as they lived close to the top of the fishing,
all the rest of us, myself included, had tacitly accepted
this as a matter of fact. Nowadays the whole of this
region is a vast watercress bed, and anyone looking
out of the window of the train, when passing over the
viaduct, would never realise that there was, or ever
had been, a river there at all; but in those days there
were two streams above, as well as below, the bridge,
meeting a little way up and stretching as one, for a
quarter of a mile to the end of the fishing.

We had all of us come on occasions as far as the
hatch below this final stretch, but, in the belief that
the water above was a blank, had always turned back
when we got there.

On August 31st of this year, the last day of the
season, I found myself at this hatch at about six o'clock
in the evening. I had got four fish averaging 1¼ lbs.,
but it had been a bad rising day, cold and windy. At
six o'clock it suddenly turned warm and calm, and I

was sitting on the hatch smoking a pipe before going home, when I thought that, just for fun, I would walk up to the end of the water. I expected nothing, and had half a mind to leave my rod behind and saunter up with my hands in my pockets. I got over the fence and strolled up on to the bank unconcernedly, and, as I did so, from one weed-patch after another there darted off a series of two-pounders racing up-stream like motor-boats. I dropped like a stone, but the damage was done. I just sat there cursing the day I was born and myself, not only for having lost the chance of a lifetime—for the iron-blues were begin-ning to come down thick—but for having left this gold-mine undiscovered and untouched for two years —and to-day was the last day of the season ! If there had been any handy way discovered of kicking oneself physically as well as mentally I should have been un-recognisable when I got home. Every fish was under the weeds long ago, and I might just as well pack up my traps and clear out.

There was an old broken-down footbridge about a hundred yards above me, and I thought that I would go up to it and explore the reach beyond, more with a view to the possibilities of next year than with any hope for the present. I got down from the bank and circled round through the meadow till I got to it, and was just picking my way across its rotten planks when under my very feet I saw a small nose appear, followed by a diminutive head and the most enormous shoulder I ever remember to have seen in a chalk stream. I froze stiff where I stood, except that my knees were shaking like aspens, for there right underneath me was gradually emerging the fish of my life. I do not mean to say that I have not caught bigger fish before and since, but this was a veritable star in the dust-heap, a

Cinderella stealing out of the kitchen that we had all despised, and the romance of the thing put him (*pace* Cinderella) on a pedestal of fame from which I have never taken him down.

It was agonising work, for he swam up in the most leisurely way at a rate of about an inch in every five seconds, while I was straddled across two rotten planks, either of which might have given way at any moment, and had to pretend that I was part of the landscape. He was immediately under me when he first showed up and I could easily have touched him with my foot. What fish will see and what they will not see will ever remain a mystery ! It was then about half-past six (old time), the time of day when one's visibility is most clear, and yet he took not the smallest notice of me. He just strolled up the middle of the stream contentedly as though he were having a smoke after dinner. I can still feel my joints creaking as I sank slowly to my knees and got my line out. It fell just right and he took no more notice of it than of a water-rat. I tried again and again, lengthening the cast as he moved up, and at last he rose towards it, examined it carefully and, horror of horrors !, swam slowly after it downstream through the bridge under my feet ! It would have been laughable if it had not been so tragic. There was I pulling in the slack like a madman, and leaving it in wisps round my knees, scared lest he should see my hand move ; and he passed me by without a word and disappeared into the bowels of the bridge.

I just knelt there and swore, trying to look over my shoulder to see if he had gone down below. There was no sign of him, and the situation was painful in the extreme, for my knees were working through the rotten woodwork, and if I tried to ease myself I should either bring the bridge down with a crash or anyway evict Cinderellum for good and all.

I bore it as long as I could, and was just going to give it up and scramble out anyhow, when I saw that nose slide out again beneath me, and my old friend started off on his journey up-stream once more.

I began on him with a shorter line this time, and he took the fly at the very first cast like a lamb. If he was a lamb as he took it he was a lion when he had it. Instead of running up-stream, as I hoped and expected he would do, he gave one swish with his tail and bolted down through the bridge, bending the rod double and dragging the point right under. It was done with such lightning speed I had no time to remonstrate. I threw myself flat on my stomach and got the rod sideways over the bridge, and then the fight began. I was on one side of the bridge, and he was half-way to Southampton on the other. He got farther and farther downstream, going from one patch of weeds to the next, and digging and burrowing his nose into the middle of it, while I just hung on, helpless, waiting for the end. He quieted down after a bit, and finding that he could not rub the annoying thing out of his nose on the south side he determined to explore the north, and he began to swim up towards me. I must have been a ridiculous sight, spread-eagled on the rotting planks with splinters digging into my legs and ants and spiders crawling down my neck, vainly endeavouring to hold the rod over the side with one hand, to wind in the line with the other, and to watch him over my shoulder all at the same time. Fortunately, I must have been invisible from below, but the moment he got under the bridge he saw the rod and tore past me up-stream with the reel screaming. But now we were on even terms and there was a clear stretch of water ahead, and I was able to play him to a finish. I was really proud of that fight, for, in addition to the cramped style which I was compelled to adopt, it took place in a stream ten feet wide, half-choked with weeds, and I got him on a ooo Iron-blue at the end of a 4x point. He weighed $3\frac{3}{4}$ lbs. when I got him home, and I have always bitterly regretted that I did not get him set up, for, with the exception of an $11\frac{3}{4}$-pounder in the hall of Longford Castle, caught in the Avon by one of the family on a " local lure " (the name of which neither fork nor spade would dig from me), he was the most beautiful river-trout in shape, colour and proportion I ever saw.

V

" IRON-BLUE "

*T*HIS chapter is a digression. It is nominally in praise of a particular fly. It is in reality in the nature of an expedition to Germany, but as the two are more or less intimately associated I make no apology.

When I was a boy of sixteen at Clifton, I met with an accident at Rugby football which completely changed the whole of my life. It was treated as a concussion of the brain, which should have been well in a fortnight. As a matter of fact I found myself in a few months' time a " shell-shock " cripple, with shattered nerves and incapacitated from any hard study for a year or two to come.* In the ordinary course of things I was to have gone to Oxford, and eventually to the Irish or English Bar, but that was now effectually knocked on the head. By some lucky, or unlucky, chance, I developed a voice which was said to be out of the ordinary, and as I was full of music, and as all my forbears had been in the Church or the Law, and I was presumed, therefore, to have an hereditary ability to face an audience, it was decided that I should go abroad and learn to sing.

Just at this time my eldest brother, Conyngham, was appointed to a diplomatic post in Württemberg, which then boasted a Legation, and he and I went off together and settled down at Stuttgart.

* It was discovered later that the damage was to the spine, not to the head.

I am afraid I did not do very much work there beyond learning the language like a native. There was not very much work for him to do either, so we had lots of time to explore, and we soon found that we were in one of the finest trout-river countries in Europe. I will speak of our earlier experiences presently. It was at one of our later finds—Wildbad—that I first saw a dry-fly.

We had been brought up on the wet-fly suitable to the Dargle river in Co. Wicklow, and our horizon was bounded by the whippy greenheart and the three-fly cast, and the manipulation of the " bob." I do not believe we had ever heard of a dry-fly at that time.

The Wildbad river was a wonderful trout-stream. We used to get plenty of pounders and 1½-pounders with Zulus and March browns, and were mighty pleased with ourselves ; but one evening as we were walking back to the hotel from the train we saw a man in salmon-waders standing in the middle of the mill-pool in the town casting up-stream with something invisible to the naked eye, and just as we came abreast of him, he suddenly, for our especial benefit, got fast into something between a torpedo and a whale, and after a grand battle landed a four-pound trout. The fisherman was the late Mr. Stepney Rawson, of whom I think with eternal gratitude, for he inoculated me there and then with the dry-fly cult, and all the fun which I have had since I owe to the first lessons he gave me in it there.

Wildbad is a famous bath for rheumatism, and he was there nominally to take the waters, but on the principle of *similia similibus curantur* he spent his whole time up to his waist in the middle of the river, and the nearest the famous Wildbad water got to his rheumatism was the outside of his salmon-waders. He was a beautiful fisherman, and it was a delight to see him cast a fly and to read and mark and learn. By the same token the best casting of a dry-fly I ever saw was at Wildbad. There was a Frenchman there who had brought casting to a fine art. But he bitterly lamented to me the fact that he could not kill fish. He always came to grief in one or other of the subsequent processes. He gave me his card and asked me to go and fish with him in France, but unfortunately I lost it and I have never seen him since. I sincerely hope he got it right in the end, for he was a charming person.

The mill-pool near the station held some veritable monsters, and their supply seemed inexhaustible. The big ones kept up an average of pretty nearly 4 lbs. There were plenty of smaller ones, too, but these one despised once one had sampled dry-fly sport. These larger fish had brought " camouflage " to a fine art, for in the matter of rising they disguised themselves as dace. You would see an insignificant little ring at the edge, or end, of the running water, which in an ordinary stream you would have left alone ; but here it was just as likely to be a three- or four-pound trout. Nor could you judge anything from their lie. They did not seem to take up any particular position, and you were just as likely to get one in the race as in the slack or the back eddies. The only thing they were consistent about was their devotion to one particular fly—a small, very dark, blue dun. You might put up a March brown or an alder or a hare's ear and they remained dace ; but once the little blue dun came bobbing down the stream they threw off their disguise. It was a heart-pounding affair to stand in the middle of the pool and cast that little black-blue speck up against the light on the head of a dace with the chance that any moment you might see your rod bent double and

hear the reel scream. It was an ideal place to kill big
fish in, for the pool was large and round and there
were no snags, so that, if the tackle was sound, it
meant a long and tough fight. I have often seen a
gallery of 50 to 100 people round the mill-pool sway-
ing and shouting with excitement. This to one who
was possessed by nature of the " performing-dog "
spirit added immensely to the joy of battle. I once
landed a fish of about ¾ lb. there, and as I was taking
it out of the net to return it to the water, a red-faced
German visitor in a frock coat and straw hat rushed
at me and said furiously, " You're not allowed to take
that. It's too small. It's against the law ! "

" Yes," I said, " I know. Would you like to have
it ? "

Before I could look round he had whipped it out
of my hand, wrapped it up alive in his handkerchief
and disappeared into the blue with his coat-tail pocket
kicking about as though it was bewitched.

My brother Geoffrey and I had another amusing
experience on the beat below the town. It was good
water here and we fished it together on two successive
days. Shortly after we started on the first day we found
that we were being followed by an extraordinary-
looking individual. This was about the time when the
All-Jaeger clothing cult was at its height in Germany,
and this man surely was its prophet. He was clothed
from head to foot in woollen tights, fitting faithfully
to his robust figure. On the top of this was a wild and
woolly red beard, and on top of that again a shock of
red hair half hidden by a " three-gallon " woolly hat.
We took him to be a typical Teutonic " back to
nature " fanatic who meant getting as near to his
motto as the laws of his country permitted. He followed us up and down the bank for a day and a half,

and never uttered a word and then, all of a sudden, a stentorian voice behind us yelled out :

" I was fishin' wanst upon the Liffey an' I cot a salmon and 'pon me word I hadn't me back turned but the rats had it et on me."

Omne ignotum pro magnifico—he came from Dublin.

I had an earlier fishing experience in Germany—in Darmstadt this time—when I was a boy of fifteen. I was going out to Switzerland for the summer holidays, and I stopped at Darmstadt to pick up my brother Charles who was studying there with a German army-tutor. This particular brother was a " bit of a lad," and did not devote the whole of his time to his studies. His brilliant career came to an end later on when he was tree-ed (literally) by an indignant mob (I forget the particular crime) and only rescued with extreme difficulty by his tutor and a posse of policemen.

But on this occasion butter would not melt in his mouth. He was a model example to his younger brother, and except for an attempt at poaching and another at smuggling he might have qualified as a Sunday school teacher.

We had a day to spare in Darmstadt, and we went with one or two friends for a bathe in a lake some-where in the town. There was a bathing hut on piles to which one had to row out. As we sat drying our-selves in the sun we saw some diminutive " pinkeens " swimming about under our feet. Above our heads was a notice to say that fishing was prohibited. We swept the shore with our eyes—all clear. From the depths of one pocket came a bit of string, from another some crumbs of bread, to which we added a bent pin and a walking-stick. We dropped the bait stealthily through the floor. It had barely touched the

D

water when we heard a yell from the shore and out
shot a boat from the landing-stage full of gendarmes
armed to the teeth. In a moment the apparatus had
resolved itself into its component parts. The walking-
stick was hanging on its peg, the string had been
jettisoned and the bread (with or without the pin) had
been disposed of elsewhere. Fishing ? *Gott bewahre !*
We pointed to the notice and said we were law-abiding
folk, and had never transgressed in our lives ; but it
was a close shave.

My brother was a confirmed cigar-smoker (*ætat* 18),
and was determined not to be without them in Switzerland. If he wanted to smoke cigars at St. Moritz he
must smuggle them in from Germany. I am certain
that the smuggling was of far more interest to him
than the cigars, which, as he probably knew, he could
get as cheaply on the other side. It was a tragic affair.
In those days we wore ulsters with hoods at the back,
and when mine caught his eye he had a brain-wave.
I was to smuggle the cigars across the border in my
hood and he was to smoke them afterwards. I quite
realised that I was a catspaw, but welcomed it as an
easy start in a life of crime.

I shall never forget the tense excitement of that
customs examination. It was almost too much for me.
We got on board, off went the train, and with a vast
sigh of relief I threw myself back against the cushions.
There was a spluttering, crackling noise at the back
of my neck, and an agonised shout from my brother—
the Corona Coronas had gone west !

The Württembergers and Badensers were, in those
days at any rate, far the best of all the Germans, and
the Wildbad people were a delightful, unsophisticated
lot. The booking-clerk at the railway station was a
typical specimen. He was a most amusing old chap

and a great friend of ours, and we kept him well sup-
plied with trout. The next two stations to Wildbad
are Calmbach and Höfen, and we were continually
going by train to one or other of them. We travelled
first-class for about sixpence all told, and this entailed,
more Germanico, three tickets each—one for the
journey, one for first-class and one for the *Schnell-zug*,
and it took about five minutes, each time, of head-
scratching and pencil calculations before he could
work out our fares, though he must have been issuing
tickets for both places for the last thirty years.

At Höfen I one day had a bit of bad luck and a bit
of good luck. I was stalking a fish and caught my knee
in the cast, and pulled the fly deep into my forefinger.
It was in right over the barb, and refused to respond
to jabs of blunt penknives or blunter scissors, and I
had, finally, to wind in and walk off to the station to
wait for a train back to Wildbad. Just on the offchance,
I called at the inn (the whole place had probably no
more than a couple of hundred inhabitants in all) to
ask if there was a doctor or chemist or other handy-
man anywhere in the neighbourhood, and by a lucky
chance found there an eminent surgeon who had come
to spend a quiet holiday at Höfen. He got it out for
me in half a minute. Nowadays I always carry in my
fishing-bag a spare Gillette razor-blade for such
emergencies, and of course the only time in the last
several years that I qualified the " always " by leaving
it at home, a friend of mine got a Variant firmly
embedded in his nose. Perhaps it was just as well, and
Providence knew best, for he found a doctor fairly
soon, and preserved his good looks. It might have
been a case of *Varium et mutabile*, so far as the said
looks went. I should certainly have operated on him
if we had been in the wilds.

The plate-layer and signalman (combined) at Höfen was a bosom friend of mine, and we often sat by the side of the line and had our midday meal together. I knew the dialect intimately from long sojourn, and he was first-class company. His small son followed me like a retriever up and down the river, carrying my bag, to the envy of all the others. He was certainly going to be a professional fisherman when he grew up, but I expect he got killed in the war. Those were jolly days in South Germany before the curse fell on the country.

There was a fish between Calmbach and Höfen who knew me so well that he nodded to me each morning when I came along. He had good cause. He lay just below a small weir, and I hooked him every time, and every time snapped off my fly in him. When I got him at last, I found a fringe of dark blue duns round his jaw, which did not seem to have worried him in the least. There was another old friend who rose in a little bay just above a bush which grew down to the edge and out over the water. It was just the right place for a big trout, with the current sucking all the food into his mouth, and insects dropping off the wall above his head. It was almost impossible to get a fly over him, owing to the tree and the wall and the set of the current, but he was such a heavy riser I stuck to him day after day. I got him at last, and he was six inches long ! In any other water one would have found him out as a fraud long before, but at Wildbad, where the four-pounders rise like dace and the six-inchers like whales, you never knew where you were.

There was a famous eight-pound fish which lived behind the band-stand opposite the hotel in the centre of the town. I had heard of him but never seen him, and I often used to pitch a big sedge in the evenings over the spot where he was reputed to lie. He never responded to the dry fly, so one day I waded down from above and put a big " Zulu " or " Butcher," or something of the sort, over the place, and suddenly there was a tug and a tremendous commotion in the water, and I thought he was as good as in the basket. Alas! no such luck. I saw him for an instant. I had in reality hooked a ¾-pounder, and he had dashed out after it like the cannibal he was. We saw one another at the same moment and never again. He was, I believe, eventually got by someone, but how, where, or when, I never heard.

The most amusing fish I ever caught there was a town resident. He lay immediately under the back window of a sausage shop. The houses go right into the river in this place, and he lived a life of luxury and majestic ease, and had grown to an enormous size on the refuse from the Wurstshop. The proprietor and I had many conversations about him across the river. He used to lean out of the window smoking, and spit confidentially on the head of his protégé, and wish me good luck and express complete scepticism as to my ability to get him. He became apoplectic with amusement when I made my first shot at it. There was a network of telegraph wires right along the street behind me at exactly the distance my line required to reach the far side. I felt the " chug " on the rod and heard the " ping " of the wire, and turned round to see the cast spinning round the nearest wire like a Catherine-wheel. I remember shaking my fist at my fat old friend at the window, and telling him that some day or other I would walk into the shop and lay his pet trout on the counter as a present for him. I had many attempts at getting my line across, and I tried it day after day till at last it was humorously and gently hinted to me by the policeman that I was seriously interfering with the traffic.

However, one morning we determined to stick to him till we got him. My brother was just as keen upon him as I was, and we chose the dinner-hour as being a time when no German who was not a lunatic would be abroad. I experimented for a quarter of an hour and found there was a place, and just one place, where I could stand and get a fly out by shooting the line. I was so triumphant I could have called out the sausage-man to see the fun, only that he was at dinner. The first cast did it. The Sybarite was entirely unsuspicious. He had had liver and lights and other " Delicatessen " showered on him for years, and when he saw a fat March brown (no little blue duns on this occasion !) fly hard into the wall above his head and drop insensible on to the water, in front of his mouth, he very naturally swallowed it. I am sure he was the most surprised and indignant fish in Germany, for he had never faced insult or danger in his life. He gave one mighty roaring splash and raced down-stream. My brother was so excited that he vaulted over the railing into the water without thinking—it was above his waist, but no matter—and netted him in a comparatively short space of time. He was a disappointment. Under the wall he looked a Hans Sachs ; in the basket he was a Beckmesser, for instead of 5 lbs. he only weighed 3 lbs. That, however, was not the point. The triumph was that we had eluded the telegraph wires and impressed for ever on the mind of the sausage-man the invincibility of the Briton.

Wildbad was unquestionably the best water we fished in Germany. It was also extremely well managed by the town, which looked upon it as one of the attractions for visitors. It turned out that not long after we had discovered it, it was also discovered by the late Mr. Coggeshall. He, seeing its possibilities, volunteered to the authorities to put it into good running order both as a fishing-river and a business proposition, and this offer they very wisely accepted. The result was that it became the best stretch of public water in the country. Bad Boll may have been better in its day, but I do not think it had come into existence as a club at that time, though my brother and I were well acquainted with part of it. I met Mr. Coggeshall for the first time at the Flyfishers' Club a few years ago, and he said to me :

" The last time I saw you, Mr. Greene, was at Höfen in the year so and so, and you were fishing the bridge-pool with an Alexandra ! "

I owned up. It was a true bill. But in this case it was not the Irish poaching instinct. Like Shamus O'Brien, " the craythur was young, he didn't know what he was doin'." I had not heard of iron-blue duns in those days or been warned off Alexandras.

We fished many other streams in our Stuttgart times. Württemberg was full of them. The first we ever tried was at a place called Urach. I can still see the big fountain in the middle of the cobbled street and the big, jolly landlord with the red beard—he was the image of the Emperor Frederick—and the sunlight which is always associated in my mind, as a permanency, with the German summer.

It was late spring the first time we tried it. We had ordered an odd set of flies from London at haphazard, and had not a notion what to put up. I believe anything would have done, for we got seventy fish that day between us, averaging a pound or thereabouts. One of the conditions was that the fish were to be brought back alive, for economic food purposes, and the wretched boys who acted as porters were worn out hurrying back with the wooden buckets, emptying them into the Brunnen and sprinting back to us. It is a good many years ago now, but I remember we got them nearly all on a Zulu.

I shall always thank Urach for another thing. It provided me with one of the most perfect examples of the German journalistic procrastinating idiom I ever saw. I have lost the cutting from the Württemberg paper, but it ran, roughly translated, as follows :

" Yesterday there broke, in the town of Urach, the famous Kurort patronised by His Serene Highness the Grand Duke of Saxe-Weimar on his hunting expeditions and famous for its wine-grapes and cider-apples, at half-past seven in the evening, at the house of Johann Schlegel, the much-respected butcher, formerly member of the town council and greatly beloved of his fellow-citizens, at the corner of the Alt-Markt, where the Ochsenstrasse enters, fire out."

I scarcely dare to breathe it, but the same idiom has unconsciously stolen, via America, into our own newspapers, and many a " spicy par," ignorant of its parentage, tickles me teutonically in the ribs with its belated verb or substantive.

After such a start we were naturally game for anything. We had tasted blood, and we looked out for fresh hunting grounds and tried a lot of other rivers. There was a place called Nagold, where there were fifty grayling to one trout, and which I chiefly remember for a battle which I had with a Bremse. A Bremse is a species of horsefly about as big as a partridge and with a noise like an aeroplane. " Bremse " is also the German for a " brake," and no conglomerate collection of rusty old cattle-trucks brought up with a bang outside Ballymacrafferty could ever approach in sheer

WHERE THE BRIGHT WATERS MEET

volume of raucous sound the voice of the Bremse on the war-path. His bark is worse than his bite, simply because he prefers cattle, but his mere presence is the most shattering thing to the soul of a fisherman that ever came out of Hades.

This particular devil had pursued me all day. It must have been the same one, for there never was more than one at a time. Every time that I stalked a fish or crept to a likely cast he " zoomed " at lightning speed in front of my nose or through my back hair, and every time without exception that I rose one he violently assaulted me in the face. Most people have been hit in the eye by a cockchafer. Multiply that by five hundred and imagine yourself racing round Brooklands at 120 miles an hour at the same time, and you will adumbrate to yourself faintly the impact of a Bremse. I had been reduced by the evening to a state of foaming hysteria, and then, just at sundown, as he was making a final attack on me, he happened to catch sight of my brother, shifted his eye off the objective for one infinitesimal moment, and flew into the landing-net. The greatest testimony I can bear to his size is that he had not time to scramble through the meshes before he was flattened out into a pulp. I can remember dancing on his corpse with a sort of berserk fury, to the intense astonishment of my brother.

These same Bremses were associated with the beginning of a very imperfect day—in fact, the most humiliating experience we ever had. We were on a river, the name of which I have forgotten, and which we afterwards abandoned for reasons which will be obvious. It was Mayfly-time and the heat was terrific. We had not been on the water two minutes when we found ourselves enveloped in a swarm of colossal flies. My brother yelled : " Hi ! I'm in a hornets' nest," and I

yelled : " So am I ! " and we both bolted for the
village. Here the blacksmith reassured us by saying
that they were not hornets but Bremses, and that
they were quite harmless and that if they did bite you
it just swelled up for a week, and then you were all
right.

Anyhow, we determined to treat them with contempt, and we fished blasphemously all through the
day and had wonderful sport. The Mayfly was thick
out, and it was merely a question of picking your fish.
We filled bucket after bucket, and sent them back to
the landlord at the inn.

As we sauntered up the river in the evening we saw
a crowd of people on the bridge and imagined that
they were out to see the sport, and we looked as modest
and as obliging as we could. They suddenly leaped at
us, seized the buckets from the terrified porters,
emptied the fish back into the water and told us to get
out of the town.

The landlord of the inn came running up, as white
as a sheet, and tried to intervene, and that diverted
their wrath on to him. It appeared that the fishing was
common property, and they thought he had hired us
to get him an unfair share. It eventually became a
slanging-match between them in the delightful Swa-
bian dialect, which I enjoyed thoroughly as the storm
blew itself out. It was rather an awkward situation
for us at first, for Stuttgart was my brother's diplomatic post, and we were in duty bound not to get into
rows with anybody. I firmly believe that it was the
vivid picturing by the landlord of the appalling
devastation which would come upon the town if they
hurt an Englischer Gesandtschaftssekretär that saved
our skins. Our bones might otherwise now be reposing
in German soil.

In those days the Württembergers, and, indeed, all
the South-Germans, were extraordinarily kind to the
English. They treated us with the greatest courtesy,
and seemed to have a real affection for anyone from
England. We had, in fact, a privileged position among
the other foreigners, and badly some of our young
bloods abused it. When I left Stuttgart many of them
were in prison for various futile idiocies, such as tearing
up benches and throwing them into the Feuersee,
knocking policemen's helmets off or flooring railway porters. There were a good many of the worst
English riff-raff in the town, typical " remittance-
men " from home, and, as I subsequently discovered,
Stuttgart had one very immoral side to its character,
but I was too young in those days to appreciate
this, and providentially saw only the happy side of
everything.

We had some delightful young countrymen there,
all the same, who made up for the others—Arthur
Haggard, the well-known soldier and writer, who was
there when we arrived and made everything smooth
for us and showed us all the ropes ; " Reggie " Lister,
later H.B.M. Minister at Tangier, where, alas ! he
died, one of the best and most amusing fellows in the
world ; and Ouseley Fitzmaurice and others. The
last-named came out as a boy of seventeen, a great
dandy, immaculately dressed, very grown-up, and
perfectly charming. We ragged him perpetually on
the score of his youth (we being about a month older),
and ostentatiously refrained from offering him tobacco
or beer, and talked down to him with bewildering
success. On one occasion, when we had all lit up
cigars and had pointedly offered him a diminutive
cigarette, he leapt to his feet, and shaking his fist in
our faces, shouted that he would " smoke any damned

cigar " we chose to give him to the bitter end, and not turn a hair.

This was what we were waiting for. We arranged on the spot that we were to assemble next day at twelve o'clock at the Königsbau—the most fashionable place in the town at that hour of the day—and we would deliver the cigar, and he was to walk up and down the Königsbau till it was finished. The penalty was five marks, a small fortune to us in those days.

We all turned up at the appointed time and handed him the cigar. It was the specimen cigar, made mostly of brown paper, which we had borrowed from the window of the tobacconist's shop opposite the station. It was over two feet long, and Fitzmaurice at that time was about five feet high. It returned to the shop.

We had an almost more humiliating, if less exciting, fishing experience than the one I have described above. Alfred von Bülow (younger brother of Prince von Bülow, who later became Chancellor of the German Empire) was secretary of the Prussian Legation at Stuttgart, and he was a great friend of ours and a fervent admirer of English people and English ways.

After one expedition with us in the capacity of spectator, he had fallen head over ears in love with fishing. We sent to England for a complete outfit for him and took him off with us to try a river, the name of which I have forgotten. We rigged him up a cast and put him in a likely place—we had already shown him the elementary principles of the art—and went off on our respective beats.

It was virgin water, and my brother and I got tired of the easy job and came back after lunch with a dozen good fish each. We thought pityingly of our protégé and his envy and hopeless ambitions as we walked into the Speisesaal. Bülow was fast asleep on the sofa, snoring, and on the table beside him were about thirty large trout, lying in profusion all over the cloth. His only remark when we woke him up was :

" My stomach feels a little heavy of much eating."

Then he dozed off again, quite unconscious that the old men had been beaten by the boy.

He had thrown his flies in a bunch upon the water anywhere and anyhow, and they had taken them three at a time, and as we had made his tackle particularly fool-proof he had just pulled them ashore without bothering about a landing-net. I do not believe he ever fished again in his life. He may have determined to depart in a blaze of glory, but my own belief is that he thought fishing was a child's game, and that we had been making a fool of him all the time.

We had the higher water of the Gutach all to ourselves in those days. This was, I gather, what eventually became the upper part of the famous Bad Boll Club. It flows out of the Titisee lake and is, as I remember it, rather like a small Scottish river with a series of miniature salmon-pools and long runs, and full of splendid trout. We fished it wet, of course, and consequently never got anything extraordinary, but the average was well over a pound, and they were great fighters.

We stayed at a little village called Neustadt, far removed from the world. You could only get there by an antiquated diligence. It was quite unsophisticated and unspoiled, and the " Post " inn was a real old German Wirtshaus. Now that the railway runs up the valley, it is probably a great manufacturing town, or a Kurort, with Ausflüge and charabancs and waterfalls and restaurants. But I shall hug to my heart the little Neustadt I knew as a boy.

The landlord was an old chap called Ketterer, with

a huge bottle nose and a voice like a mad bull. The children would cluster in dozens round the Brunnen in the street to look at the trout, when suddenly there would be a roar from Ketterer, and in an instant the street was empty. I do not believe they were really frightened of him, for they used to hide round the corners, laughing, and sneak back again the moment he turned his back. I expect it was a regular game of theirs, and that " Ketterer baiting " was another form of " Cockyolly " or " I spy ! " The evenings after dinner, when dog-tired and full of good living we sat in the Bierstube and smoked and talked with the Black Forest peasants, will always remain with me an affectionate memory of the old South Germany that used to be.

I was not far wrong in my prophecy, spoken of above. I went again to the Black Forest in 1928. I wish I had not gone. I went to Neustadt. The " Post " was there still, and the Bierstube, though now exalted to a Speisesaal, was full of the ghosts of old friends. Ketterer's grandson was now the landlord and he welcomed me as one of the fishermen who were still remembered. But the Neustadt of our day was no more. The meadow at the foot of the hill below the " Post," where Conyngham and I started our daily pilgrimage, was meadow no longer. A factory was in possession, and under the bridge above it the cast-off boots and ancient tyres rubbed shoulders in the bubbling water. Cinemas were round the corner ; doctors and dentists were on the telephone ; and the omnibuses awaited the daily tourist at the railway station.

There had been no railway at Neustadt in our day, but we had seen it in the making ; and as the train that evening took me back to Freiburg I looked far down from the heights of the canyon walls into the depths below and remembered the days when we used to come the other way, and drove through the flowery Himmelreich in our old two-horse diligence, and climbed this same dark Höllenthal, and passed the time o' day to the Italian workmen and the engineers, and looked up at the mighty cliffs and wondered if they would make good in our time.

The biggest fish I ever saw in those parts came—there were two of them—out of the Titisee lake itself. This was a remarkable case, for the Titisee was supposed to hold nothing but pike, of which I have caught dozens trolling from a boat. But one day a pleasure-party brought in two beautiful trout of 3 lbs. each. They had found them swimming about on top of the water and had knocked them on the head with an oar.

It appeared that some years earlier someone had turned in a lot of brown trout as an experiment, and they had never been heard of again till these two turned up. They were supposed to have had some disease of the gills which brought them to the surface, but I cannot guarantee the accuracy of this. That they survived at all was a miracle, for the lake was literally infested with pike.

I was bathing there one day when something hit me a violent blow on the leg, and cut it rather badly. I was sure, from the look of it, at the time that it was. a monster pike which did it ; I had swum over the same spot dozens of times and knew there was not a snag of any sort in the water, and even now I am half inclined to believe it.

There was an old Gasthaus at the end of the lake, and one summer it was practically monopolised by a large party of English people. Dr. Playfair and his wife and daughters were there, and Nigel his son, a small boy at the time, but up to anything in the way of mischief; Sir Edgar Boehm, the sculptor, and his family; Dr. Henry Bond (later Master of Trinity Hall); and a lot of undergraduates and other Cambridge people, and a large contingent of my own family. We were all very young, in spirits anyway, and we made things lively.

We rigged up a lawn-tennis court somewhere and somehow, and we got a big india-rubber ball from Freiburg and played water-polo in the old flat-bottomed boats that collapsed if you sneezed in them, and worked off one practical joke after another on everyone indiscriminately. I still have a vision of Dr. Playfair (a very short man) waltzing down the passage with a colossal dummy dressed up in clothes stolen from my uncle's room, and of that same uncle (David Plunket, later Lord Rathmore, of House of Commons fame) threatening him with sudden death. The dummy, at the moment, was on the way to precipitate itself into the bedroom of one of the visitors whom we suspected of being too " quiet." We leant it up against the victim's door, and knocked and hid round the corner. We heard a mild " Come in ! " altered to " Herein ! " when there was no response, and after a long interval we heard him open the door, and then a crash and then there was a prolonged silence. We thought it must have knocked him insensible, and we crept up to see. He was sitting on his bed, paralysed with laughter, gazing at the figure on the floor, with the tears pouring down his face. He was the most popular ruffian in the crowd from that moment.

With all this we were the best of friends with the aborigines and the other pensionnaires. They entered delightedly into all our jokes, and one of them, a journalist, actually wrote an article for the *Schwäbische Merkur*, called " Jung-England am Titisee," which was a really beautiful appreciation of youth and high spirits.

It was here that I first came across " absolute pitch " in music. There was a Prussian officer staying in the hotel with whom I made great friends. He had been shot in the right elbow at Gravelotte and could not bend his arm, yet he played the piano beautifully ; but what impressed and bewildered me most about him was that he could tell me, without looking at it, the name of any note I played on the piano. I thought at first it was a trick, but he survived every trap I laid for him. I had never heard of " absolute pitch " in those days, and looked on him either as a freak or a conjurer.

My brother and I were, I firmly believe, the first people to introduce lawn-tennis into Germany. There was an old Thiergarten (otherwise a Zoo) in Stuttgart, which had two or three very mangy monkeys and about three-quarters of an eagle on a chain as its sole stock-in-trade. But it had a skating-rink approximately the size of a lawn-tennis court, and we rigged up an apology for a net, marked out the lines and invited some of our German friends to an exhibition match and afternoon tea. In less than no time the Thiergarten became a social centre, and the " quality " flocked to it in crowds—amongst them, if I remember right, the famous (later) Graf Zeppelin ! It soon got too big for its boots, and eventually we migrated to Cannstatt, just across the Neckar, and made a grass court by the bank of the river, and got proper tackle over from England.

It became a regular society craze, and I can remember the untimely fate of a certain charming officer who became so light-headed with enthusiasm that he turned up one afternoon in flannels and a black-and-white

E

blazer, and was promptly court-martialled. Nothing
daunted, he returned to the fray and played in the full-
dress uniform of the Blue Uhlans, frock-coat, helmet
and all, until one day, in a paroxysm of acrobatics, he
caught his spur in his watch-chain and dislocated his
knee, and that was the end of him. I can guarantee the
truth of this statement, for I saw him do it.

The cult did not long survive him, and its decease
was equally amusing. A boat with some very amateur
oarsmen who were watching the game close to the
bank suddenly upset, and my brother waded out into
the water to drag them ashore. The matrons promptly
gathered up their skirts and departed in a body. " The
Herr Gesandtschaftssekretär Greene had gone into
the river and got his clothes so wet that one could see
his legs through his trousers," and lawn-tennis from
that moment was " off."

All this has apparently little to do with the special
fly on the Hampshire Bourne, but Rawson's little dark-
blue dun at Wildbad was its father, and the son has
been the best friend of Rawson's pupil ever since.

Every fisherman has his pet flies. I do not mean
local flies, but flies of regulation pattern which he is
prepared to back in any water. It is surprising how
few you need. I only want half a dozen, in the following order—iron-blue, red quill, pale watery dun,
ginger quill, olive quill and hare's ear. At Hurstbourne
the Whitchurch dun also was invaluable on a sunny
day. I do not count sedges and orange quills and
variants, which are more or less fancy flies and all
right in their proper places ; I am speaking of the
ordinary duns and quills which come up in the day-
time and which are our stock-in-trade, and of course
I refer to the winged fly and not to the spinners and
blue uprights and tups and hackle-flies generally.

If I was to be limited to one fly for the rest of my life I would scrap all the others and stick to the iron-blue quill. It is not merely a Test fly, for I have caught a two-pound trout with it in a little Scottish burn, casting it dry on chance up-stream into a likely place. There used to be a superstition that the iron-blue was a bad-weather fly and only useful in a thunderstorm, but my experience is that it is the best of them all on glass-smooth water in bright sunshine. In fact, it is often the only fly they will take in such conditions, and it is certainly the only thing they will look at when they are smutting. If you pick up a smut and examine it closely you will see that it has the identical metallic blue-black colour of the iron-blue. It is quite probable that the trout look on them as the smaller and larger edition of the same fly. This is borne out by experience. Everyone knows the " fisherman's curse," which in spite of its diminutive size monopolises the whole attention of the fish when it is coming down. They treat everything else with silent contempt, and suck down the tiny smuts greedily. The iron-blue is the only fly of regulation pattern which they will take in these circumstances.

The most fast and furious week-end I ever had was on the late Col. Grove-Hills's water on the Kennet at Ramsbury at Whitsuntide in 1921. The Mayfly was up and going strong on the Friday. We arrived there at luncheon-time on the Saturday, and were on the water about three. There was not a sign of Mayfly—it was over, but from that moment till I took down my rod on the Monday night there was a steady rise of fly, which never stopped even for half an hour. It was more than steady, it was brilliant. It was a " Mayfly " rise of duns. There were gingers and olives and pale-waterys, floating down in crowds. But the fish were taking no notice of them. They were picking out the iron-blues every time. During the whole of those three days I never changed my fly once till the sedges and blue-winged olives came on in the evening. It is a commonplace to see the iron-blues on the water in dark blowy weather, but on this occasion the heat was almost tropical—we were burnt as black as coals by the Monday—and there was not a breath of wind, and yet they wanted nothing but the iron-blue for breakfast and luncheon and dinner, and often for supper, too.

This does not apply merely to the Kennet or the Test or the Bourne, but to trout-water anywhere. The big Black Forest trout would have the dark-blue dun or nothing. If your fish is a big one, it does not matter whether he is a Rooshian or a Prooshian or a Frenchman or an Englishman; he would rather have the iron-blue at any time in any weather. I do not mean that you cannot catch them with others, but if you have to stick to one, or pin your faith to one for the rest of your life, then stock your box with iron-blues.

There may be some physical reason for it. They may be very fat, or very tasty—why else should they be so partial to mere hors-d'œuvres like the smuts?—or they may look very luscious against the light; whatever it is the trout could not have a greater affection for them than I have.

It is, no doubt, imagination, but the iron-blue always seems to me to be happier and keener and to have better manners than all the rest. He is an aristocrat, a prince on the wing, far above the world of under-water hacklers, as he sails down serene on the stream, oblivious to wind or rain or sun, above board in his every thought and ready to work for you again and again till he disintegrates and falls to pieces from very exhaustion.

If an olive or a ginger sticks in a tree or snaps itself off in the air, it is invariably its fault, and it is treated to the appropriate language ; but if the iron-blue in some strange moment of apparent forgetfulness lands me in a tight place, I apologise to it, for I know that I am to blame.

In the early days at Hurstbourne I did most work with the olive quill and Little Marryat, but it is interesting to see in my diary that in 1903 " at the very end of the month a small (ooo) very dark, almost black, blue dun was the only fly," and from that moment the pre-eminence of the iron-blue was established for good and all.

In all the years I fished the Bourne I never caught a fish upon a Wickham or saw an alder or a March-brown upon the water.

VI

THE BEATS ON THE BOURNE AND THE TEST

IN 1904 the Hurstbourne fishing reached its high-water mark. I wish to emphasise this fact, for reasons which will appear presently. There is no reason why there should ever be a high-water mark in any fishing. The very name implies a turn of the tide, and, granted that nature or man does not take a sinister hand in the game and dry up the waters or poison them with pollution, the level of excellence of a trout-river need never vary appreciably. I have known the Ramsbury water on the Kennet for many years, and I can never remember it as anything but first-rate. There is a definite reason for this. Its virtues are due to inertia. The word has a common-sense value in this case, as will be shown presently, and what was common sense for the Kennet was common sense many times multiplied for the Bourne. As I think of 1904 and that little river, and how she treated us and how we treated her in return, I hang my head with shame and ever shall do so. *Post equitem sedet atra cura.*

On looking through my summary for this year I see that " There was a fish to be found on the rise somewhere at some time of the day, and I had no blank day," also that " a very dark-blue dun, small, or, better still, a small iron-blue quill seemed irresistible, and the old stagers would come up at it when they would not look at anything else."

My bag for the season was 193 fish, weighing

271¾ lbs. This amounted to an average of 1½ lbs. each.
You people who cross that viaduct on the Salisbury
line look down at the little silver ribbon below you
and take off your hats ! Not to me or any other of
her rods—she treated us all alike—but to the little
Bourne, laughing down the valley like a child from
school, blissfully unconscious that she is a heroine.

How many of you have sat by the side of some river
five times her size, and gazed in admiration at the
monster lying beside you on the bank ! What is he ?
A pound and a half ! Ye little gods and big fishes,
and that was the *average* of the Bourne in a matter of a
couple of hundred of them ! And remember that this
was day-fishing—we never bothered about the evening
rise.

As in the previous year, the last day of the season
was the best—seven fish weighing 13 lbs. Here they
are : 3¼, 2½, 1¾, 1½, 1½, 1¼, 1¼. I like to think of that
last day, for we never saw its like again.

Three of these—3¼, 1¾ and 1½—were the three I
spoke of on page 1. They were all lying in the little
stream below the viaduct at the place where the cattle
generally crossed, and were rising merrily. I had extraordinary luck with them, for I got each one in turn,
without disturbing his neighbour. They were feeding
side by side in a row, with the biggest one in the middle.
The water was quite shallow and as clear as gin, and
I could see every spot on their backs. So far as I
remember I had only three casts at them in all. I was
naturally going for the big one in the middle first, and
just as the fly was coming to him one of the smaller
ones darted in and grabbed it from him. This happened twice, and in both cases the luck stood by me,
for I managed to get each in turn down-stream and
play him to a standstill below me ; so I was able to

leave the big one undisturbed and get him, too, in the end.

There was nothing particularly noteworthy about it as a performance beyond the fact that the stream was so narrow that there was no free water to speak of and lots of weed to make up for it ; but I had learned very young the virtue of keeping out of sight of the fish hooked in cramped water, and I never gave them a glimpse of mankind till the end. Also, by the way, I never had occasion to shift my ground during the whole operation. I just knelt where I was, and the first two obligingly ran down past me and stayed there, leaving the coast clear for number three. All three were in perfect condition, all fought like heroes, and there was hardly enough water to cover them in the place of their rising.

I should like to emphasise the fact that these, like the other Bourne fish, were all " wild " fish who had never tasted horse-flesh in their lives, had possibly been spawned within a few yards of the place where they were caught, and had grown to maturity in that upper mile of water. They were yeoman stock. (No wonder they looked thoroughbred.) Their fathers and mothers had made their living for generations on the same weed and gravel farms.

These ribbons of water were regular diamond-mines. You would get a two-pounder in a few inches of water, where you would swear that there was not, and could not be, anything bigger than a sardine, and would imagine that he was the one and only one in the place ; then you would stroll up another twenty yards, and lo ! another and yet another ; or you would come back in half an hour, and there would be a new one pretty nearly as big as his predecessor in the old place. Where they all came from will for ever remain a mystery. There was not an inch of water which was not clearly visible and which you could credit with hiding any secrets.

The two little streams below the viaduct are perfectly open, as one can see from the train, and free from trees, but the fishing is not so easy as it looks or sounds. Not only was there no cover, the cattle keeping the grass eaten down, but there was generally a strong wind blowing up or down the valley and whistling through the arches of the bridge. Putting a fly clean upon the water from a long distance in that narrow channel was ticklish work. Catch your fly up in the grass and drag your line across the top and it was all up.

The left-hand stream runs through a tunnel under the embankment and the hatch below the exit is memorable to me, not only for many luncheon-hours, but for the circumvention of one particular fish.

There were a few odd pounders in this hatch-hole, one of which I used occasionally to get, but, though the pool was deep and transparent, and though plenty of fly came down it, I never saw a sign there of anything remarkable. Yet I felt in my bones that there was a big one in it somewhere. The middle of the pool was clear, and I could see every stone on the bottom, but down one side from the end of the coping there ran a series of small stumps, or piles, which stuck up out of the stream, and round which the water swirled and churned. It was, of course, an obvious place for a " master " fish, and I had put a fly over it dozens of times, but had never seen a fin. It was my sixth sense that told me he was there. So one evening I lit a pipe, lay down, and waited and watched. Nothing happened for a quarter of an hour, and then I saw one of those little bubbly rises which we all know so well in rough water, those manifestations which we hope are real rises and know are not. There was nothing to distinguish this from any of the others except the " message " to one's brain. I waited a bit, and then I saw it again a little farther to the left, and a moment later I saw a gentle undulation in the smooth water of the back eddy round the pile. Then I got to work.

There was just one place where the line did not drag, as I knew by experience, and I put the iron-blue fair and square into it, and before I knew where I was he had taken it, rushed round the pile, and snapped me off. I felt much the same sense of dazed fury that I once had when I walked into a lamp-post (my eyes being engaged in watching a dog-fight) and knocked my pipe out of my mouth—and one of my teeth with it.

It was all over for that day ; but I got him the next evening. I tried him with the iron-blue, but he had had lots of opportunity of quiet meditation on iron-blues, as there was one sticking in his jaw when I landed him, and he treated it with contempt ; so I put up an olive quill, and he came to it quite unsuspiciously. I was prepared for the pile game this time, so the moment I hooked him I pulled him out into the pool and then lay as flat on the ground as I could with comfort, and managed to keep him out of danger till he was landed. He was $2\frac{3}{4}$ lbs. What I want to know is, why was he invisible to a trained eye for so long in spite of the fact that he lived in an obvious place, and why did he never show the sign of a rise or any other life until the particular days when I set myself to see and rise him, and saw and caught him ? Was it my fault, and was he see-able and catchable all the time ? I do not believe it. I feel now, as I did then, that it was somehow communicated to the fisherman's sixth sense that he was there and would rise that day. Perhaps sometimes one leaves one's sixth sense at home.

I had an amusing and instructive experience with a $1\frac{1}{2}$-pounder not long ago at the lower end of this tunnel-stream. He was the most confiding creature I ever saw, so much so that when I got tired of kneeling I stood up openly, and he kept on rising at me just the same. I must have put the iron-blue over him fifty times ; forty-five times he must have risen and forty-five times I must have missed him. Everybody knows the *decrescendo* of enthusiasm of the missed fish. He came at it at first like a lion, and I pulled it away from in front of his nose. He did it again and again, and I did it again and again, and each time he looked a little more hurt than the last. The routine was so regular and dependable that I tried experiments in timing the strike. He was lying in six inches of water, and I could see every scale on his body and every wag of his tail. A more hopelessly incompetent performance could not be imagined, and finally he got bored with it. His enthusiasm gradually flickered out ; from darting at the fly he betook him to rising slowly and gently opening his mouth ; thence from spurning it with his nose he came to mildly annoyed tail-wagging, and finally to sullen contemptuous passivity. I flogged at him for about ten minutes, but he was apparently in a sound sleep. Then I put up a red-quill as a complete change, and he literally leaped at it and hooked himself at once—for I am prepared to swear I was incapable of saving him the trouble. The thing is, of course, a commonplace, but it was interesting to watch, for the game was played under my eyes in a gin-clear shallow by a fish which deliberately provided a demonstration for my benefit.

I see that on the same day (August 29th) on which I got these three together in the little viaduct stream I foul-hooked a " monster " just below them, and lost him. This talk of big fish lost was not all a matter of imagination, for the Bourne, as I have said, was a " sight " river, and you could see your opponent every time. In the Kennet during that 1921 Whitsuntide, I lost seven fish in one day, which simply tore off upstream into the weeds with the casting-line under water and either snapped me off or hung on there, impervious to hand-lining, till I had to break away myself. I like to believe that they were " whales," and I have no sort of doubt about it from the feel of them, but I have nothing to prove it. But you could tell the weight of a Bourne trout within an ounce or two before you ever put a line over him. I put this particular one as somewhere near 4 lbs.

I see, too, that on that same day I rose the " flyrefuser " opposite Savage's cottage. He was Savage's and Sharkey's especial enemy, for he lived in their garden, so to speak, and treated them with a contumely that drove them to desperation. I firmly believe they would have sworn off fishing for the rest of the season if thereby they could have circumvented him. I just as firmly believe that he had no fear of any human being, and was tickled to long life with the whole series of lures and snares and contraptions which they fired off at him. I often used to have a shot at him as I passed by, but beyond a wink and a laugh he never took any notice.

I do not know how he happened to forget himself on this occasion, but I do know that it was at the ironblue and that it was such an event that I had to go into the cottage to tea and " rub it in." I had once, about a month before, caught a fish which I thought

was the " fly-refuser," a horrible long thing with half
the upper jaw gone on one side and long rows of
shark's teeth, had labelled it " *Sharkeiius ferox*," and
had left it on their table with suitable triumphant
remarks and insults; but I am afraid the laugh was the
other way, for the next time I was passing they took
me sadly and silently to the well-worn spot in the
garden hedge, and there, in the same place, was the
old playmate whom they had once risen when they
were boys, smiling and unconcerned as ever.

I will quote one more day as typical of the sport in
1904 : " July 28th, eight fish weighing 14¾ lbs.
Simple murder to-day . . . came home early as I had
got four brace."

I see, too, that on three separate days I hooked and
lost a big fish between 3 and 4 lbs., whether the same
fish or a trio I do not know, in the deep water above
Savage's. I got that season two fish of 3½ and 3 lbs.
respectively, three of 2¾ lbs., three of 2½ lbs., and sixteen of 2 lbs. and over.

That is the best testimony to the little Bourne. I
was only one among several rods, and what it did for
one it did for all.

As I said earlier, the fishing also included a good
mile of the Test, running from the head of the Longparish Common water to the G.W.R. railway bridge
at Whitchurch. The upper part, or Tufton water, was
excellent in the early days, and held beautiful fish, but
it went back steadily each year until it became hopeless.
There was no apparent reason for this, but I am quite
sure that it was due to pollution up above.

The main body of the water passes down what is
now the main Test, and carried the damage with it—
to such an extent that the bottom of the river probably
became more or less foul. There was also a carrier

which branched off below the top hatch. This ran over clean gravel which filtered it to such an extent that by the time it reached the open stretch I speak of, it was comparatively harmless. Wyld was of opinion that this carrier was probably the old bed of the Test, and he strongly advocated the diverting of the water down it once more, for a while at any rate, and I agreed with him. If the sun and the wind could get to work for a spell on the old watercourse, it might renew its old powers. But the real thing to do was to remedy the pollution, and when that is brought up one is always faced with the question—who is to pull the chestnuts out of the fire ?

I hold firmly to the opinion that wherever you see either black or yellow fish there is pollution. There are all sorts of theories about black fish—that they are fish which have been hooked and badly man-handled before being returned to the water, and the like—but wherever there is pollution you will find both, or either, black and yellow trout. Both are sluggish, like sick men, and both are poor to eat, the yellow ones especially being oily in taste and positively nasty. The water above Whitchurch was full of black fish, and that immediately below of black ones and gold ones, and pink ones as well. We used jocularly to attribute the variety to the jam factory above, and say that it depended upon their individual preference for black-currant, apricot or strawberry.

The yellow colour to which I refer is a peculiar one. There are many " gold " trout which are splendid fish ; these were white-gold and semi-transparent, and looked as though they should have been in a bowl on a lodging-house table. The stretch of " coloured " water is a perfectly defined one. The farther the river flows down the fewer black fish you see ; on the other

SAWMILL SHALLOWS

hand, the extreme upper water of the Test, close to the source, holds, or used to hold, nothing but clean fish. I know this from experience, for I fished those upper waters when the late Admiral Stopford had the beat.

I spoke earlier of the joys of running across undiscovered water, and this upper part of our fishing in the Test furnished me with another happy experience. I could see it deteriorating day by day under my eyes, and I had finally made up my mind to abandon it when it occurred to me that it might be worth while to examine the little carrier which turned off at right angles at the top hatch. I had not thought of it before, because it disappeared almost at once into an impenetrable jungle of trees and hedges which skirted the meadow beside which it ran. I followed it down, more to pass the time than anything else, and walked along the water-meadow, catching only an occasional glint of water through the undergrowth. Suddenly I came upon an open hatch, and below it, with a short interval of cover, a stretch of open water about 200 yards long, edged with wild cress and with a golden gravel bottom and a number of really beautiful fish lying in the open. The water was very smooth, and there was a feeling of repose and remoteness about it as though it belonged to some enchanted garden and the fairies would come to bathe in it at sundown. Everything was slow and sleepy. The fly floated down asleep and the fish rose with closed eyes. But they were wide enough awake when they were hooked. One, or maybe two, were the limit I got then or at any subsequent visit, for the news travelled like wildfire once we started. No one seemed to have discovered the place and, though it is quite well known now, I had it all to myself at that time.

I have no intention of describing the Test or Bourne in detail throughout their length—a tedious catalogue of beats to a reader who does not know the water— but there are, or were, a few spots which I should like to dwell on simply to show their infinite variety. Take, for instance, the lowest beat of all below the Heronry where the Bourne flows into the Test. There were two streams here, broad, fast-running and well stocked. The river, or rivers, had by that time lost their Bourne character and were both Tests. One of them was divided into two by an island at the lower end, so that there were three Tests here, and you could wade up each of them, and work your way from one feeding fish to the next. Some people have a preju-dice against wading and look on it as a sacrilegious and selfish device to spoil the water for others. My experi-ence of the Bourne is that it does not do the slightest harm and has no effect upon the rise, and if that applies to a miniature stream like the Bourne it is even more true of the broad waters of the Test.

It did not matter what time of day you turned up on this beat, there was always something worth while for you. Even if you caught the two big fish you saw there on a Monday, on the Tuesday you would find two more, which had probably come up from the Longparish Common water to take their places.

These deputies were often very amusing. The beat below was divided from ours by a wire fence across the stream, and the big fellows had a way of taking up their positions either under or immediately above the wire. Apart from the gamble as to which side you would find them, or whether they would creep up or drop back, there were the intense excitement of getting your fly straight across the stream and the palpitations of the heart which go with terror of the drag and the sight of your enemy dropping slowly back with his eye cocked suspiciously at that little dun that moves in such a funny unorthodox way across his nose. Six inches did it; if he receded that much you were a poacher. But sometimes you were rewarded. I remember following one of these jibbers on his backward course with curses and fist-shakings, having wasted a futile perspiring half-hour over him, and as I leaned exhausted against the wire a better than he swam slowly past me up-stream, brushing my waders as he went, wagged his way with great deliberation to pleasant casting distance, took up position, rose and obligingly swallowed my fly as soon as I asked him to. It was the most hospitable apology for the other's bad manners. I have seen half a dozen big fish lying under this wire one beyond the other. There was always a chance of some one of them and the moral certainty that there were others above.

From here the Bourne twisted and turned like a spiral as far as the Jackass Hatch (so called because it was reputed to be the only place in England where anyone had ever found a dead donkey), and thence in a straight line right up to Savage's cottage. It would be hard to say which part of it was the best; but there were one or two spots which were specially interesting owing to the conditions. There was a cascade in the middle of a clump of trees behind the church, where the park broad water empties. This was another " discovery." We used to stop at the barbed-wire cattle fence below the trees and go round and start in again above. But one day I crawled under it and stole up under the trees. I found the place full of fish. It used to be great fun then and later, trying to switch a fly round the trunk of one tree into a miniature pool at the roots of another or even to pluck a fish from the very jaws of the cascade. It was a capital variation from the open river.

The saw-mill shallows below Savage's were just the reverse of this. They were the principal spawning-bed of the river in winter and almost as full of heavy trout in the summer. You had to wade up to them and fish very far off, and you had to coax your fish down-stream if you got him. It was a most interesting experience to stand high up and far back on the bank, when the light was right, and watch another rod at work. You could see dry-fly fishing as a demonstration there to perfection. I often took friends and sat with them there and watched someone else working the shallow, and I am certain I was far the most excited of them all.

There were two other " stunt " beats in the upper water, one a stretch below Savage's which ran under thick trees and gave one all the variety of sport and language that one could wish for ; and one above the viaduct. This was the most unorthodox apology for a trout-stream that ever asked to be taken seriously. Only the Bourne could have mothered it.

It was in reality a narrow artificial channel running from one patch of watercress beds past another, and emptying into the main-stream just above the viaduct. It was flanked by a low wall on one side and a high bank on the other, and if ever an earth-work of man contained every devilish freak of nature it was this bank. The water itself was about six inches deep throughout its course, and not more than four feet across, but that made no difference to the trout. They looked upon it as a sort of sporting race-track, or at least that was the impression they made upon you nine times out of ten. They were almost impossible to approach. If you stood up you were like a poplar on the skyline, and if you tried to wade you sent a wave of information ahead of you, and in either case there was a general post ; if you compromised by kneeling down on the bank, you were lost in the big weeds that rose over your head and swamped you. You generally developed into an inglorious reptile, stung by nettles, harried by wasps, maddened by caught-up flies, crawling through thistles and briars and chucking your fly anyhow, anywhere, with a splash that would frighten a tortoise.

But occasionally things would go right, and when you got a fair shot it generally meant a rise, for, as is so often the case, fish in uncanny places are far less guarded than those exposed to temptation in the open. If you were lucky enough to coax your friend downstream you could move up and try for another ; but as a rule he shot off up-stream, and then it was like hell let loose. The other fish just tore up and down the narrow channel like racing-motors. I got to know the actual musical note of the hum of their scurry-by. When this happened it was no use trying again for a few hours, and I was only too glad to drop down off that infernal bank, thankful that it was hopeless for the rest of the day.

Just above this was the hatch below the top-water where I got the big 3¾-pounder the year before ; I once saw Dr. J. Brunton Blaikie lie down on his face beside it, roll up his sleeve, and lift two two-pound fish in succession out of it in his hand. He was a tall thin Scotsman, so we waited till he put them back.

Between the channel and the main-stream there was a still pond-like straggling pool which we called " the lagoon." This was a remarkable evening-rise stretch, and the big fish flocked to it from afar at sundown. I think of it now with indignation—I have never lost

so many good fish in succession or played the fool so
consistently as here—and with a homesickness akin
to that of the days when I left Ireland to go back to
school; for the lagoon is all that is left to tell the
traveller to Salisbury that here there once was a river.

As I look from the window of the train my heart
aches, for there below me I see acres and acres of
watercress beds, laid out with a ghastly precision
between long lines of concrete walls, like some nightmare sewage-farm, with only the remnant of the lagoon
to tell me that here I once had the sport fit for kings;
and the solitary pollard-tree, sole survivor of the wreck
of old days, standing like a sentinel to mark the spot
where on August 31st, 1903, the little Bourne and the
little iron-blue and I made merriest of all.

To me those white bones are the grave-stones of a
romance, a romance between her and me which I
helped to bury. She looks up at me as I pass above her
on the bridge, and waves to me sadly and never says
a word of reproach. She knows I am sorry. I did not
build the stone-walls that make her prison or cage her
with the iron trolley-bars—God forbid! But I helped
to dig her grave.

VII

THE TRAGEDY OF THE BOURNE (1905)

IN the winter of 1904-5 we re-stocked the water. We put 2,000 yearlings and 500 two-year-olds into the Bourne and Test—chiefly into the former—and 200 Loch Levens into the broad water below the park. What happened to the latter I do not know. They either resolved themselves secretly into the ordinary brown trout, as is their wont, or departed from the Bourne in disgust. We never saw them again.

It is easy to tell what happened with the others. It is written for those who run to read. In the light of bitter experience I could preach a world-polemic against overstocking. Common sense is all that is needed, and yet when it comes to replacing fish that are caught the average fisherman becomes a megalomaniac and a glutton, blind of one eye and staring through the wrong end of the telescope with the other. Let us take a few simple facts and put them side by side, and we shall see the tragedy of the Bourne and how it came about.

The Bourne, as said before, was a small narrow stream, so shallow as to be wadeable in short waders throughout its course, except for a quarter of a mile of the broad water and 100 yards by Savage's cottage.

The number of fish taken out in the season by all the rods combined could not, at the highest estimate, have exceeded 1,000. There was practically not a pike in the water ; I never saw one of any size. There were a number of spawning-beds, models of what spawning-beds should be, scattered through the river, and these were covered with trout in the winter. The hen-fish lays on an average about 2,000 eggs. Grant that only 1½ per cent., or 15 in 1,000, or even only 1 per cent. if you will (Mr. Donald Carr of Blagdon puts it as high as 3 per cent.), of these survived and grew up, there would be, in view of the numbers on the spawning-beds, hundreds more fish brought into the water than ever the rods took out. And yet we put in 2,000 yearlings from outside at the time of year when the big fish were all away and they had the river and whatever food was in it all to themselves, and 700 semi-adult to adult fish as well !

We asked for trouble and we got it. Nemesis pursued us from that moment. The season of 1905 was awful. It was one long series of gales and bitter cold and " not a fly on the water." I quote from the diary : " There was no surface food for the fish, and, in addition, we were rather overstocked "—when I read this I do not know whether to laugh or to cry—" so the big fish never came into condition, and got to look like miserable eels. The young ones got all the little food there was." In the last sentence can be summed up the whole indictment.

As everybody knows, the chalk-stream trout, when he grows to a size of authority, takes up his quarters in a comfortable place with his tail against a stone, or a pile, or a patch of weeds, where the current will bring him down the food without any bother on his part. This beat he will hold against all comers and here he will stay at his ease, sucking in whatever the gods send him, without ever moving away, except to chase off interlopers or make an occasional tailing excursion into the weeds after shrimp, and returning in each case to his old stand to take up position again. If the food comes along in plenty, he gets strong and fat ; if it does not, he starves, for he will not go to look for it.

That was the pitiful history of the Bourne from 1905 on. The figures tell the tale :

1905 : 170 fish weighing 218¾ lb., the best of them being taken at Bransbury Common several miles down the Test.
1906 : 180 fish weighing 189 lb.

One could see the game being played under one's eyes—the old fish in position slowly wagging his tail and waiting for the millennium, and the little two-year-olds darting about in front of him and snapping up everything eatable before it reached him. One saw him early in the season chasing them away furiously and dropping back to his stand ; and then, as time went on and he grew weaker, his rushes would become fewer and shorter, till at the last he just lay there enervated, inert, blue and blind, and one lifted him out in mercy in the landing-net and put an end to him.

I remember one in particular. He was slowly swimming about in circles on the top of the water, black and stone-blind. I netted him out, and when I took him in my hand he gave a horrible cry like some warm-blooded animal. No doubt it was something to do with pressure in the air-passages, but it made my blood run cold, for it felt like a vivid impression of the curse which had descended upon the water.

Signs of *saprolegnia* appeared at the end of this year and the beginning of 1906, and we shot a good many bad fish and managed by luck to eliminate it before it had got too far ; but the real cause of it all was contained in the report from Fishmongers' Hall, to which we had sent a typical " diseased " fish : " This fish died of starvation."

What a pitiful picture that brings to the mind ! When I think of those gallant gentlemen with whom we fought so often, and who beat us far oftener than we beat them, bright, bonny and bursting with health and spirits, and remember that we let them starve, with all the misery it must have meant to them, it comes between me and my sleep. The vision of those old warriors, lying on the top of the water, blind-eyed and emaciated, haunts me to this day.

The explanation was patent and so was the solution. Lord Portsmouth was, as usual, ready to do whatever we agreed should be done, but we could never get a unanimous decision from the rods. To make assurance doubly sure, I asked Hugh Sheringham down to report on the river, giving him no information as to our respective views. His report was that the river was badly overstocked, and that a good half of the fish ought to be taken out and disposed of. He could have come to no other decision, and if his advice had been followed the Bourne might still be the best trout-stream of its size in the kingdom.

But it was not to be. The mischief went on, the fish died of hunger, and the proud little Bourne fell from her high estate and went to the workhouse.

Here is an average quotation from 1906—naturally the damage would be more apparent the year following :

" Aug. 3. Got three miserable fish, 1 lb., $\frac{3}{4}$ lb., $\frac{3}{4}$ lb."

We had to look the other way and call $\frac{3}{4}$ lb. fish " pounders."

" Aug. 6. Same thing. River deteriorating day by day. Fishing a farce. One fish, $\frac{3}{4}$ lb."

I do not claim any credit for superior knowledge.

I was guilty of the original sin like all the rest, but at least I repented. I would earnestly, nay passionately, urge the owners of the smaller, and even the larger, trout-streams, to think twice before re-stocking. When you eliminate the pike you leave nature free to make up the deficit caused by the work of the rods. If the spawning-beds are good, you can leave re-stocking to her. Colonel Grove-Hills told me that in all the years he had the Ramsbury Kennet he never put in a fish, and yet that water to-day is full of them. I have never seen a black fish there and hardly ever a lean one, once the season was in swing. It is, of course, deep, heavy water, and there would probably be food enough to go round even if fresh fish were put in, but nature preserved the balance, and always will if you leave her alone.

It is a strange thing, particularly interesting to me, that the physical economics of singing are precisely the same as these. There is a popular belief that the trained singer fills himself up with breath as full as he can, holds on to it like grim death, and lets it out in infinitesimal quantities in the making of vocal sounds. As a matter of fact, he does not want any breath at all beyond what he happens to have normally in his lungs at the moment for five out of every ten phrases that he has to sing, and every extra barrelful he imbibes helps to strangle him and all his means of expression, tone, rhythm, thrill and diction. Nature is essentially an economist. She hates to be either hustled or crowded. Whether you sing a song or fish a river your greatest enemy is overstocking.

Let the man who is about to re-stock ask himself a few questions :

Has the river good spawning-beds ?

Has he extirpated the pike and other coarse fish ?

If he can answer these in the affirmative, let him then ask himself :

How many fish does he take out of the water ?

Do the spawning-beds hatch out enough to fill the gaps his rods have made ?

If his bag was smaller this year than last in the matter both of weight and numbers, was there nothing to account for it ? Was there a poor rise of fly throughout the season, and were many more fish tailing than before ? Was there less shrimp in the weed ? Was the water low ? Were there any signs of tar or other pollution ?

If, at the end of it all, he decides that fewer fish are coming into the water naturally than he takes out artificially, and that the average of weight is going back, let him look at his spawning-beds and his weeds and bring his family to birth in healthier conditions and feed them better as they grow up. There would not be such infant mortality or so many starving tramps under the hedges. Above all let him not turn in others to divide the little that there is.

The tragedy of the Bourne is a striking example of what it costs to go one better than nature. If we could have doubled the volume of water and planted it afresh with weed, and turned in a few million shrimp, we might have made another inexhaustible Kennet. But the Bourne was not made that way. It was a wise schoolboy who said, " Man cannot live on stones alone." No more can a Bourne trout.

That was thirty years ago. Think of it ! Thirty years to emerge from the swoon of starvation to which we sent her. And she can never be the same again ; for up above the viaduct the trees and the flowers and the snipe and the wild bees are gone and the great silver trout with them, and the place thereof knoweth them no more.

VIII

I PREFER to pass over 1906 in silence. The size and condition of the fish were pitiable. They were starved and took anything you chucked in in sheer desperation. " Fish in hundreds, but not one good one." The only ones that were worth taking were in the Test. I hardly fished the Bourne seriously at all ; it made me too sad. I had one interesting day on it—or rather bit of a day—when I explored the tunnel-stream at the far side of the viaduct. It was all overgrown with trees, but I could just flick a fly in now and again and I got four, all in fairly good condition. This day, and the catching of a $2\frac{1}{4}$-pounder in the Tufton (Test) water were the only bright spots in the whole of the season on our own fishing.

The best sport I had was when I went to Bransbury Common with Wyld. Bransbury Common is one of the most romantic spots in the South of England. It is a huge water-meadow common, with cattle wandering all over it, and a haunt of wild birds. It is one of the rare places in this country where the short-eared owl has been known to breed. This is the owl who is reputed to attack you if you come near when the young birds are hatched. We had a great bit of good fortune with regard to him, for I asked the late Mr. Hugh Elliot, a very keen bird-man, down specially to find him, and find him we did and had a good look at him and his wife at close quarters. Not only this, but while we were lying in wait for him, we saw a cuckoo pay her legendary visit to a reed-bunting's nest, and actually found her egg there afterwards. That was about the only bit of luck that 1906 held for me.

This Common feels as remote from civilisation as the Sahara, though the resemblance ceases there, as you discover if you try to cross it without waders. It belongs by prescriptive right to the snipe and the duck, and man is an outrage on the landscape. It lies between the Test and the little Bullingdon river, both first-rate, and there is a small carrier running almost at right angles from the former, which is as deep as it is intimate. It was ideal dry-fly water in each case, for the banks were good going, there were no trees, it was admirably keepered, and all three beats were full of grand trout. I do not know which of them was the most exciting, the big stretch by the hut on the Test with the shallows in the day-time and the Ham-carrier in the evening ; the Bullingdon river all day ; or the little cross-piece connecting them where you lay flat and looked stealthily round the curly corners. They were all so good and the fish were everywhere so finely educated and so sturdy in physique that you were always keyed up to your best ; but I think the little cross-stream was my favourite, not only because the other rods did not trouble about it much, but because I love the little winding streams as I love cocker spaniels.

This particular rivulet had flat banks on one side and bulrushes on the other, and the stream itself was about ten feet across at its widest. It was very deep and it wound in and out in letter S formation, with short stretches and rounded corners ; and round each corner you crawled with your heart going like a sledge-hammer, knowing that as you poked your nose over the top you might see the fat ring bulging out from under your bank. As often as not it was so close to you that it seemed impossible to cast at all without showing yourself. Many a time I have lain sprawled across one of those corners, watched indignantly from under the bulrushes by some evicted three-pounder as my legs trailed in his late habitat, with my stomach glued to the crumbling bank, holding on for dear life to a thistle with my left hand and chucking and chancing it with my right. Whether he was rising right or wrong and whether I got him or not, he was always a good one. I never saw a bad fish in this particular carrier.

I think I like Bransbury Common best of all the upper waters of the Test. It is true that in those days there were a good many rods on it, but it was all so wild and stormy—the wind in the Test valley is a permanent institution—and romantic in its atmosphere, and the fish were so in keeping with it in their wildness that it felt like some Robinson Crusoe island, and one was drawn to a rival rod for sheer companionship. The only drawback was that Wyld used to eat most of my luncheon. He would draw a banana ascetically from his pocket and say that he could never tackle anything in the middle of the day, but in the end he generally had the luncheon and I the banana. The Common had a predatory atmosphere which was infectious.

There were two fish there which I never forgave. One was a three-pounder, who rose regularly in the open a hundred yards or so below the hut. I must have hooked him a dozen times in the various days I was there, but I never got him near the net. He was such a consistent riser that I was positively indignant when at last he sulked and would not come up any more. We were so intimately associated that I looked upon him as my private property, always on hand to provide me with a prize-fight, and when one day I arrived and found he was gone—for I never saw him again—and realised that some poacher with a hackle fly had robbed me of him, I regretted that I was only a guest of the club.

The other fish was a big, hilarious, salmon-like humorist who lay with his tail against a stump under the far bank half-way between the little fall and the shallows. He was exceedingly good-looking, and he knew it ; also the fly invariably dragged six inches before it reached him, and he knew that, too. I have never seen a fish more acutely, and yet comfortably, aware of that acid test than he. He sucked in the non-draggers and fairly shook with laughter at the draggers. Nothing put him down. He was as safe as a house with that infernal little swirl acting as policeman. When I think of the hours I wasted over him, without once rising him, even with a late sedge, I grind my teeth.

1907 was a maddening season. " There was not one quiet day on the Bourne in the whole of the four months, and the sun never shone. It blew without ceasing in a series of interminable gales in one's teeth till casting became a weariness of the flesh and fine work was impossible, and one's hand seemed to lose its cunning and to have forgotten all it ever knew ; mackintoshes all day and cowering over fires every evening." Truly England has to pay for its privilege of being mothered by the Atlantic. The water was very low and muddy, and full of two-year-olds and very little else. I got 175 fish weighing 196 lbs., but the only two that I saw which were any good eluded me. As they were the only two worth taking in the river,

I expect they were the best-trained pair in England. Every rod that came on the water probably made a bee-line for them.

Wyld, however, got one of them. This particular hermit lived just above the donkey-hatch, and was as inviolable, apparently, as St. Senanus. Wyld was strolling miserably up-stream with his friend, Ernest Pain,* and was being eloquent upon the rapid approximation of the Bourne and every other river to Mephistopheles. Just as he approached the hatch, he saw a shoulder heave in the well-known place. He sank tremblingly to his knees, threw a fly jaggedly above the rise, rose the fish, struck and landed it. He was semi-hysterical with delight, and he and Pain spent ten minutes slapping one another on the back, weighing the fish progressively in a succession of half-pounds (he was actually 2 lbs.), debating the advisability of setting it up for the sake of posterity and bewailing the absence of champagne by the river-side. Suddenly they became aware of a sinister presence. Another rod was coming across the field to the familiar spot. He was far too absorbed to see them. As he approached the river he bent double, dropped to his hands and knees and crawled to the place Wyld had just vacated. He stole along, every nerve quivering, face and body tense, stared long and blankly at the water, sagged gradually, stumbled to his feet and began to shamble off. It was too much for Wyld. He leaped up, whirled the fish round his head and shouted, " Too late, old chap ! "

There was a horrid monotony about the whole season, and not a day of real interest except one at Bransbury Common on August 28th, when I got eight fish weighing 10½ lbs., and saw a sunset which I shall never forget ; and one day, August 22nd, on the

* Author of *Fifty Years on the Test.*

Midleton water at Longparish, then belonging to the late Mr. Colin Patrick, which for sheer enjoyment was, I think, the best individual day I have ever had on any water. I got ten fish weighing 17½ lbs., and put back three of 1¾, 1¾ and 1½ lbs. respectively, as they were not in perfect condition. This was the only other warm day during the whole summer, and the effect on man and beast was magical. It was one of those days of wild exhilaration that every dry-fly man knows, when his sixth sense is wide awake and he can tell by intuition where the next rise will be, when the water seems to palpitate with life and the big fish which have lain hidden all the year come up to the top, when the duns float down thick and steady and stand out clear upon the shining water, when the swifts flash by you and every bird sings the rondel of joy :

> " Le temps a laissé son manteau
> De vent, de froidure et de pluie."

When you know, too, that you will cast right, and strike right, and play right and land right ; all the subconscious things that bubble up with blue water and high spirits, and fine weather, and green fields, and green trees, and golden mimulus, and make you want to shout because you are alive and in the open.

There was not one fish that day that did not fight like a lion, but there was one particular hero. I was wading up the deep water of the old Test—it runs in two branches here—the banks being too squashy for comfort, and was having splendid sport. There were plenty of rising fish to cast for, but something told me that I should do well to put a fly into a run under the bank just ahead of me. There was nothing rising there and it was apparently empty and a waste of time, when so many others were patently asking for it. The result fairly frightened me. My line had hardly touched the water before it was tearing up-stream with the reel screaming like a mad thing. He made the longest first run I ever remember with a river-trout. He took the whole of my line out and part of the backing, and was then only stopped by coming up against a weir. I expected to see him take this in his stride and hurry along to Basingstoke, but he turned back and raced down again and then up again, as fresh as a daisy. Unlike most trout, which generally exhaust themselves by the first wild rush, he kept repeating it. He was far more like a salmon than a trout, and for a considerable time I actually thought he was one, and had cœrulean visions of writing to the *Field* a description of the encounter with, and capture of, a ten-pound salmon on a 4x point and a ooo ginger-quill, dry. He was $2\frac{1}{4}$ lbs., as a matter of fact, and that will always be the best fighting weight for fine tackle. This was a " ginger " day, and I got my first six fish on the same fly, never changing it till it was worn out—none of your hackles, but winged and floating like a fairy boat and dancing up and down on the ripples from sheer delight in the sunlight and the sport.

I realise—and own up—that I am a fool to stick to the winged fly. All my experience, and that of others, goes to prove that the hackle fly is the more deadly killer. But it all depends what fishing means for you as an individual. To me every separate bit of my tackle has a personality, and I love my winged iron-blue as I love my dog. To me the hackle-fly is a ferret and the winged fly a cocker spaniel. I loathe ferrets and their dark, underground ways, and my sympathies are always with the rabbit, but to see a spaniel hunt a cover is a poem of fairplay and the chase.

Justice compels me to admit that I have modified

G

these opinions with the advance of time. My prowess with the nymph is still negligible, but my prejudices have suffered a sea-change. Nothing can take the place —for beauty—of the winged fly as he sails down upon the mirror of the water ; but all good things well done are close to beauty and the true prophet of the nymph has the right to be proud of his creed. And in this wicked world beauty must occasionally give place to materialism, for to a hungry man the trout in the basket abandoned the regions of romance when its spots began to fade, and the silver dried upon its shoulders.

There was one ferret who was an exception to my rule and for her sake I would apologise to her tribe. She was my friend. She was not carried in a bag ; she went to and from the hunting grounds in my pocket (I was grown up) and I could handle her like my dog. She would walk all over me and (I feel sure) try to talk to me.

One day, in a moment of madness, I put her under a stack to turn out the rats. Nothing happened for a long time, and then she crawled out and died at my feet—the rats had finished her. The reproach of it burns me still.

IX

HERE was a slight improvement in 1908 in everything except the weather. The days were cold and dark and dreary in the extreme. The nights were always fine and still, but with the day up came the wind. Out of the thirty-seven days I fished, on twenty-six it blew hard from the N.E. or N.W. bang in one's teeth and generally half a gale. Against this we had had a wet winter, and the Bourne, which generally rises at St. Mary Bourne, was flowing miles up the valley ; and on April 24th and 25th we had a remarkable snow-storm, which piled the drifts right up to our windows. It seemed to pick out the Test and Bourne valley, for it lay eight feet deep on the road-sides and blocked all traffic. It was so thick in Whitchurch that the liveryman could not get his horses out of the stable on the morning of the 26th. It had melted gradually, so that the river was over its banks most of the season and the fish had a fair chance.

It showed a slight improvement in the figures—167 fish weighing 188 lbs.—but all the decent ones were caught in the old reach above the viaduct, and the main Bourne was infested with small fish. I got seven one day weighing $9\frac{1}{4}$ lbs.—and put back four of $1\frac{1}{4}$ lb. each which were out of condition—and eight on another day, including a two-pounder, which was a rare thing in those times. I had a similar experience this day to one I spoke of earlier. A $1\frac{1}{2}$-pounder ran down through a hatch, and as I could not get my rod through I had to play him to a standstill from up above, and stick the rod in the ground and go round and lift him out below.

On most of the days that I went to our beat on the Test I found the water like pea-soup from weed-cutting. There did not seem to be any understanding between the owners of the various stretches. As fast as one beat in the upper water was finished another would begin, with the result that the people below had a pretty muddy time. It is extraordinary that the riparian owners, or tenants, on the great trout-streams do not take the trouble to meet and evolve a policy of some sort as regards weed-cutting and come to an agreement as to dates. The motto of England is " Always 'as been," and no doubt we shall dodder along as before, and the poor devil with the solitary holiday will spend a blasphemous Saturday smoking on the bank and cursing the " laitue " soup and the cooks who made it.

The wind and the cold were indescribable. On two occasions Admiral Stopford came over from Overton and each morning we started out chuckling with delight that the wind was S.W. and the sun warm, and each time, as we spoke, it leapt round to the N.E. and blew a gale, winding up on the second day with a thunderstorm and torrential rain. It is no wonder that the diary says : " Iron-blue all day," though that is a libel on the little gentleman.

I had one really wonderful day (August 10th) on the Longparish Common water, the stretch immediately below ours on the Test. This is the water of which Hugh Sheringham spoke in *Trout-fishing*, where there is room for three rods to wade up the water abreast and have all the elbow-room they want.

SUNDAY AFTERNOON (WYLD AND I)

I got seven brace weighing 18½ lbs. and I put back several others. But it was not merely the numbers that made the day such a success. It was the wonderful feeling of space and the knowledge that there was practically not a single rising fish that you could not get to. The whole beat, with the exception of a small bit at the lower end, is a " deep " shallow negotiable in salmon waders. On every side of me, and as far ahead as I could see, were long weed-patches with a trout feeding at the head of each of them, and occasional gravel beds, and odd piles with ripples running round them and head-and-tailers cruising in the tails of the pools. This valley, where the Bourne and Test join, is quite wide and full of duck and snipe and red-shanks. When you are standing up to your waist in the middle of the river you feel you have the world to yourself.

There was nothing particularly notable about any of the fish I got that day, but I had a curious demonstration of the tricks which light and the angle of vision (if that is the right technical name for it) can play on one. I had often sat on the high bank above the water at the top end of this beat and ground my teeth in envy as I looked at the giants reposing beneath me, so near and yet so far, with that cold-blooded wire fence to tell me to keep my distance. There were three of them which I put down as averaging 4 lbs. each. They had their respective positions at the head of the patches of weed, and the diminutive three-pounders did not dare to poke their noses round a corner. There they lay majestically, shining transparent against the golden gravel, sucking in the flies lazily and looking pityingly up at me as I told them what I would do to them if they would be kind enough to swim up another dozen feet into respectable water, and how a certain

small friend of mine of the name of " Iron-blue "
would soon knock their fat complacency out of
them.

I actually did get one of them on this day, and he
weighed 1¾ lbs. !

In most cases one can tell the weight of a visible
fish within a quarter of a pound, and one knows how
much smaller they look in the water than out of it,
but here it was the exact opposite. I suppose that when
one looked down upon them perpendicularly, as in
this case, the water acted as a magnifying glass against
the gravel bottom.

I had one interesting day on Bransbury Common on
August 22nd, and got a few good fish, but I chiefly
remember it for some trick-riding by Mr. Granville
Bromley-Martin on a bicycle. He and I had ridden
over in the morning more or less successfully. He
hated bicycles more, and knew less about them, if
that were possible, than I did, and there never was a
man so pleased to see home as he was to see Bransbury
Common. It was Wyld's bicycle, lent in ignorance,
and was a three-geared affair, and during the day
it slipped back somehow or other to first speed.
Bromley-Martin had not the remotest notion of what
a gear was, or how to change it if he knew it, and I
shall never forget the vision of an old Eton and Oxford
blue wandering about the road in circles with the
wheels racing and his feet tearing round, to his abject
bewilderment and terror, till he finally toppled into the
river in a burst of profanity.

I did not take a rod on the Bourne in 1909, partly
because it made me too sad and partly because there
were now three small (not in size) children to think
about with views of education to come, and I did not
feel justified in going in for expensive luxuries.   I

occasionally fished it with one of the others and I have fished it many a time since, but to all intents and purposes this was good-bye to my old friend.

However, I arranged with Mr. Myles Bailey of Leckford to take a rod on Chilbolton Common lower down the Test, about seven miles from Hurstbourne. The ownership of this water was in dispute at the time, being claimed by the Ecclesiastical Commissioners on the one hand and by Mr. Myles Bailey, as lord of the manor, on the other. The decision was given some years later in favour of the former, but it had not then been brought into court and you could fish it if you were prepared to fight for it. There were, as a matter of fact, one or two assaults on, and by, the rods, but there was no Donnybrook in my case.

It is a miniature Bransbury Common, water-meadow and wild, with a bit of the main Test and a mile or so of carriers. It is just below Wherwell, one of the prettiest villages in Hampshire, and the carrier skirts the Priory and passes under the bridge on the Winchester road at a place called Butcher's Mead. It was nobody's business to keeper it, and the banks were in a shocking state. It was the most exhausting work I ever knew, for one had to wear salmon-waders, and almost every step one took along them one sank in thigh-deep and had to haul out with a sticky " schloop."

The fish were few and far between, but were as wild as hawks and beautiful specimens of the real Test fish. The yellow-bellied strain had not yet been introduced, and any one of them might have served as a model for a museum.

The most interesting tussle I had there that year was with a three-pounder at the lower end, interesting in that he was the reward of long patience coupled

with good luck and as a demonstration of the trout's
protective armoury.

He lay close under the near bank in the main Test,
but, unfortunately, in order to get within distance of
him one had to cross a plank over a small ditch which
ran almost parallel with the river and made his part of
the bank into a peninsula. He would rise freely and
jubilantly when I was standing on the bank below the
ditch, but the moment I put my foot on the plank he
stopped. There was no question of his seeing me, for
the plank was so far from the water that only his rings
were visible to anyone crossing it. It simply meant
that when one stepped upon it, one shook the peninsula
in some infinitesimal degree and the shock was communicated to the water around him. Whatever the
explanation the result was always the same—down he
went. Time after time I crawled across that plank and
wormed my way on my stomach, like a red Indian, to
the casting-point, and lay there looking at the blank
water and kicking myself for a fool. Once I touched
the peninsula he never stirred again.

However, one day I had a stroke of luck. The distance below the ditch was too great, apparently, to
reach him with any rod, otherwise I should not have
wasted so many precious hours over the peninsula
approach. But on this particular day it was blowing
half a gale from the S.W., and by some extraordinary
freak of the wind my line shot an extra six feet and
landed the fly bang in the middle of his ring. He was
quite unsuspecting—his home had been burglar-proof
hitherto—and he took it without a question. I did
not think I had a chance either of striking or holding
him with that length of line, and when he ran clear
through the big bank of weeds in the middle of the
river and out on the other side and half-way to the

village to look for a policeman, I made sure it was all up. But the luck held and the tackle with it, and I got him down again and actually back through the very place in the weeds he had gone through before. He had not much fight in him by then, and he came to the net quietly enough, but it was a great tribute to the man who made the tackle and to that particular sou'-wester squall.

On August 3rd I had another wonderful day on the Midleton water at Longparish—6½ brace weighing 22 lbs., twelve of them caught between eleven and two. There was a delirious rise on and the water was fairly teeming with big fish. As fast as I got one another would come up in his place. I put back fifteen of over a pound, and I went home at three o'clock. For intensive sport this would be hard to beat.

The Bourne valley is one of the most beautiful spots in the world, but in the matter of weather it was, in those days at any rate, downright detestable. I see in the diary that the chief event of the summer of 1909 was " the discovery of the North Pole by Commander Peary at Hurstbourne Priors, Hants "—an infantile hyperbolism which nevertheless fairly expressed the concentrated venom which inspired it and which was more sadly and simply stated in the final word of the summary : " Fires every night and bed packed with blankets." The wind whistled down that valley—for the accursed thing never blew up—like a myriad army of razor-blades cutting you to the bone, and not on one day only, but day after day, until the wretched season blew itself out.

The end of it was worthy of the beginning and the middle. I went up to Altnaharra in Sutherlandshire to fish with Sir Charles Stanford. This was in August. There had not been a drop of rain there for weeks.

The water was dead low and the river nearly dry and the loch practically a non-riser. We got a few sea-trout in it, but it was stormy and bitterly cold with great black clouds over our heads, and, as everyone knows, that puts loch-fishing out of the range of practical politics. Meanwhile, there was a heat-wave in Hampshire. I had been asked to go for a week's salmon-fishing and grouse-shooting in Ayrshire, but had had to refuse it, as I was captain of the Hurstbourne Park cricket club, and had to be back there for a special match against a team brought by Merric Bovill. The day I left Scotland the weather broke and the spate came, and when I got to Hurstbourne I found the match was off and the North Pole had taken up its quarters there once more.

I only fished eleven days that year, and got thirty-seven fish weighing 53½ lbs. These were practically all taken in the Test. They might have been taken in Siberia.

X

SOME INTERESTING EXPERIENCES IN 1910

IF it was hard to do justice to the season of 1909, words are quite inadequate to describe that of 1910. The diary says :

" It is no wonder that the character of the Briton seems to be changing. He never sees the sun from January 1 to December 31. If he turns communist and rejoices in the humiliation of his once-respected country he can hardly be blamed. His crops are ruined by the rain, his health by the bitter cold, and his temper by the raging winds and Cimmerian darkness, which allow him neither rest nor light. It is generally understood that it is necessary for a man's health and well-being, physical and mental, that he should get rid of the poison in his system by perspiration. I will defy any man to have turned a hair in the dog days of 1910. Day after day the same story—pitch darkness all day with gales from the N.W., masses of clouds, sheets of rain, bitter cold and never a glimpse of the sun."

I had a rod on Chilbolton Common again, but I hardly ever went there on account of the weather. Seven miles' journey on a bicycle, to arrive drenched to the skin and paralysed with cold—it was too much even for me.

As before, the best days I had were at Longparish.

August 1st at Midleton, six fish weighing 8½ lbs. ; August 22nd, at the same place, six fish weighing

10½ lbs.; and August 25th, on Col. Sneyd's water (Longparish Common), five fish weighing 9¼ lbs.

On the first of these days (August 1st) I saw a most interesting thing. I had slept the previous night at the Patricks', and we had gone out duck-shooting at 5 a.m. (It is a wonderful valley for duck and all wild birds. I once saw Wyld get a duck, a teal, a snipe, a partridge, and a rabbit there in five successive shots.) At about seven o'clock I came to the hatch where the new Test rejoins the old river. There was a mist over the water, and as I came near I saw vaguely that the stretch ahead of me was boiling with rising fish. They were tearing about like mad things, snapping up something on the surface, and as I came closer I saw that the water was covered with flies. They were coming down so thick that in the back-eddy above the hatch there was a thick pudding of them, surging round and round in a black-grey mass. I picked up a handful of them and found that they were big flies with an iron-blue body and a gauze wing, not duns but shaped like a small house-fly. There is a certain fly on the Test rather like them, which bites you, but this was a freak. I have never seen such a rise, evening or otherwise, on any river, and I have never seen this particular fly before or since. There was something uncanny about it. I felt as though I had surprised Nature when she was sure that the world was asleep.

The surfeit did not seem to interfere with anybody's appetite, for later in the day I got the six spoken of above and put back half a dozen more. The entry for August 22nd is significant—"Any fly good enough."

The Midleton water, when it was on its day, was unbeatable. If I ever had wanted to show a foreigner the best view of an English trout-river I should have taken him there.

There was a beat of fast water at the bottom, then a hatch and then a long canal-like stretch of slow deep water, very like the Kennet, in which you might see a dozen two-pounders in position one after the other. This was hard to fish as it ran very slow, and there were trees above your head, but it was all the more interesting, and there was no fear of your depleting the stock. I remember once seeing a queer-looking fish floating down on the surface here, and hooking it out with my net and finding to my amazement that it was a grayling. It was still alive, but in such an advanced stage of disease as to be almost unrecognisable. Goodness knows where it came from or how it had got there, for at that time a grayling had never been heard of in the upper waters of the Test, and this one was miles up from the grayling region, and was floating down-stream.

Above the "canal" comes the school-meadow, and that is one of the places I like to dream about. It is a broad shallow, wadeable throughout, with stones and weed-patches scattered in profusion, and at the top of each a big trout, and along the far side was a bank of flags and in every hollow there was a two—or may be three—pounder asking for trouble. There was one monster at the top of this stretch who remains a blot in my memory to this day, for I hooked him and lost him, and never in that year, or any other, saw him again. I had a clear view of him both before and after rising him, and I know he was one of my life's failures.

Above this were the reaches of the old and new Test with a big swirling pool at the junction, and then a broad stretch of that open fast water which makes the Test the king (as the Bourne is the queen) of all the English trout-streams. The whole thing is typically

English—the water-meadows, the country roads with the little bridges over the carriers, the thatched cottages, the snipe and the duck and the sedge-warblers, the flowers and the bumble-bees.

The then rector of Longparish, Mr. Parry Woodcock, is a beautiful fisherman, and as keen as he is skilled. He knew all the great fish within a mile of Longparish, and he told me of several particular celebrities, two of which I got. One was in a little winding carrier, very like the cross-stream at Bransbury and worked on the same method. He appreciated the iron-blue as much as I did, but, though he weighed 3 lbs., he was not in condition, and I sadly returned him to his home.

My brother, Geoffrey, was with me later on, home on leave from Ceylon, and we had one or two good days at Chilbolton, but the season was then practically over. His fishing has been mostly of rainbows at Nuwara Eliya, but I bring him into the story because he was a witness to a certain exploit of mine which has been received with such contumely wherever I have told it that I wish to record it as an attested fact.

I was fishing one evening in the kitchen-garden water at Wilton. I hooked a grayling, and as I brought him up to the net I saw that he was foul-hooked over the right eye. Before I could land him the point broke and I lost him. My brother was not with me on this occasion, but I told him about it when we were comparing notes afterwards. Two evenings later I was fishing in the same place, and he was beside me. Again I hooked a grayling, and again as I brought him in I saw that he was foul-hooked (apparently) over the right eye. I landed him this time and found that I had not touched him at all, but that the hook of my fly was caught in the hook of the fly which I had left in him,

over his right eye, two days before. I am quite aware
that at this point I ought to throw up my hands, but
truth, though stranger than fiction, shall prevail, and
if a member of one's own family is reluctantly prepared to corroborate there is nothing more to be
said.

Dr. J. B. Blaikie, spoken of earlier, told me that he
was once fishing for sea-trout in a Scottish estuary.
The tide was going out, and as it receded he saw that
his fly was caught up in some seaweed on top of a rock.
He tugged and tugged at it with no result, and finally
laid the rod on the ground in order to hand-line and
break off the fly. At this moment the top joint dis-
played nervous tremors, and he altered his diagnosis.
He seized the rod again and began winding in. There
was a tremendous commotion on the top of the water
all the way to shore, and he finally landed a plaice!
When the audience was very young he caught it on a
dry-fly.

The water above Midleton, belonging to Longparish
House, has the same delightful characteristics. It is
very broad and you can wade up most of it, and cast
for one fish after another as you go. The stretch in
front of the garden is one of the prettiest things on the
Test. I remember seeing a young cuckoo sitting on a
post in mid-stream here with two excited wagtails
feeding him in relays at express speed. They were so
close I could have touched them with my rod, but they
were so obsessed with their responsibilities and so
bewildered by his appetite, that they paid no attention
to me. It was an infuriating thing to watch, for he
was young enough to be very ugly and the sight of him
sitting there like a fat Caliban and opening his huge
mouth, and of the frenzied working of his foster-
parents to fill his capacious maw, combined with the

thought of what an almighty fraud he was, almost made me knock him into the river.

In a carrier to this water lay, and no doubt still lies, the cutest trout of his generation. He weighed about a pound and a half, and he was wreathed in smiles from head to tail so long as I knew him. He lay in a foot of fast-running water immediately under a barbed-wire cattle fence which crossed the stream. Half his body was below the lower strand of wire and half above, and he never varied his position an inch, but just opened his mouth and sucked in anything that took his fancy. If you cast over the top the weight of the line pulled the fly over his nose like a wild-duck alighting on a lough. The lower strand of wire was only six inches from the water, and it was impossible to cast under it. There were trees down to the water's edge on either side and the stile was within three feet of him. He was one of the few fish I have known whose castle was absolutely impregnable ; but what I admired most was his knowledge, first, that his safety was a matter of inches and depended upon his remaining in one spot, and next, his complete unconcern as he fed on in perfect safety. The whole Diggle family tried him many times, but I gather he was never caught.

In 1910 I fished fourteen days and got sixty fish weighing 84½ lbs., which was good enough.

XI

DIGRESSIONS (1911)

IN the month of May I had only two chances to fish, as I was away singing most of the time. The weather was beautiful so far as sunshine was concerned, but it was marred by a virulent east wind which lasted most of the summer. On the first of these occasions the wind turned to a N.E. gale the moment it saw me get into the train, and we sat and cowered over the fire all the week-end; on the second we had a terrific thunderstorm winding up with a miniature cloud-burst which washed clean through our gardener's cottage, nearly drowning the cat and leaving a ton or two of Hampshire mud behind it. I never got out of the house.

I wish some astrologer would tell me the sinister weather-and-traffic-regulating star under which I was born, for most assuredly it has pursued me relentlessly ever since. It is one of the few adversities which cannot be attributed to auto-suggestion, for Jupiter Pluvius and Hermes are presumably above and beyond deep or light hypnosis. All I know is that, with the exception of the Kennet, which has invariably played the game, foul weather, gales, east wind, sheets of rain, and perishing cold have dogged me all my life and fallen upon me, sometimes singly, but generally all together, whenever I have got near a river. I have suffered all things—from the thunderstorm which knocked a hole in the street outside my inn in

H

Donaueschingen to the ice which froze the line in the rings of my salmon-rod on the Dee. I am never really happy except in a Turkish bath, so that I am particularly susceptible to this outrageous type of persecution.

Deeply as I loved the Bourne and sorry though she was for me, she suffered in my estimation from her low companionship. If one lived on a river, as I did, it might be supposed that one could dodge it somehow, but it defeated me invariably. If ever it drew back it was only in order to return with greater ferocity. But what maddened me was the fact that the moment I left the house to go to London or elsewhere, the sun would come out, the birds would sing, the grass would grow and the earth would glow with heat, and this would last till I got out at Whitchurch station on my return, when the east wind and the ice reappeared as if by magic.

I remember once in a moment of lunacy starting off on a tricycling expedition (it was before the days of the pneumatic-tyre bicycle) with a brother and a cousin from London to Horsham. A more miserable way of cutting oneself with knives and lancets could not be imagined. It blew half a gale in our teeth the whole way down, and we arrived in a state of semi-collapse. In a weak moment, as we sat shivering and eating our luncheon with chattering teeth, I remarked that anyhow the wind would be behind us on the journey back, and as I spoke it gave a roar and swept round to the opposite side of the compass, and blew in our faces the whole way home.

I defeated it once with conspicuous success. I was going to Oxford for a day on the river, and as I was buying my ticket at Paddington, I said in a loud voice to a friend close by that I was just off to Torquay, and then whispered softly " Oxford " to the booking clerk.

As we steamed out of the station I hugged myself, for I saw a mighty storm racing off in the direction of Torquay as hard as it could go, and I had a glorious time in a punt. It found out the trick later, and turned back to Oxford in the evening and kept me in the house for the whole of the next twenty-four hours, but I had had my day. I have tried the same game at intervals since then with varying success, but I am afraid the weather is getting to know it.

The same applies to locomotion. The buses which I want as a rule are 9 and 33, and I am prepared to bet, at very good odds, that I can put in their exact order the prior arrival of 49, 28, 27 and 73 (often in repeated relays), before the appearance of a solitary 9 or 33 packed to suffocation. If, on the other hand, I am going only a short journey when any bus will do, the left-hand side of London going east becomes a wilderness. Buses of every denomination flow westwards in unending streams, but my side of the road abandons itself to sandwichmen and cats licking their chests. After æons of time I see phalanxes of buses pouring up my way in an unbroken line, only to find that two minutes before the whole of the inhabitants of Olympia have been vomited forth in a fighting mass; and the drivers pass me by either with set faces and " Full-up " eyes, or with sympathetic deprecatory waves of the hand, and I take a taxi. My hopes were aroused when the "pirate" appeared upon the scene; but he was soon absorbed, and I am back again at zero.

I have never been in a hurry to catch a train, but the horse of my hansom has spread-eagled upon the slippery pavement, or the fog has descended upon my four-wheeler, or my taxi has been manned by a Methuselah of eighty-five, whose engine chunk-a-chunk-a-ed along on first speed; on the top of that I have invariably been stopped by the policeman's hand or the red light at High Street, Exhibition Road, Albert Gate, Hyde Park Corner, Hamilton Place, Berkeley Street, Bond Street, Piccadilly Circus and the rest.

I have never got into a station where there was a gate to slam without its being slammed in my face when I arrived. (I once had to wait in Baltimore, Ohio, from 10.30 p.m. till 5 a.m., owing to a slammed gate and the waiter not bringing me my bill.) I never used to appear on the platform at Down Street tube without finding that the next train passed that station, or arrived at South Kensington on the Inner Circle without seeing twelve trains on the District Railway given priority of advance. I have never got into an empty omnibus in an empty street at lunch-time (when I am particularly recommended to travel) and congratulated myself on getting a short rest, but, as the conductor pulled the bell, thirty members of the other sex have flown in from the park or the roofs of the houses, and I have had to stand all the way. I have never gone into a shop when the sales were on and asked for the pair of boots which I saw marked in the window at 28s. 6d. without being told that that particular sort were really 75s. 9d. I never got into a four-wheeler (*faute de mieux*) in the middle of June in the old days but a November fog descended upon the earth, and I had to lead the horse to Euston.

I only once really scored off a four-wheeler. I was singing at a miscellaneous concert at Hanley in Staffordshire. In those days we used to stay at the hotel at Stoke, a mile or so down the hill, and drive to Hanley and back. On this occasion, when the concert was over, our four-wheeler was nowhere to be found. We all set out to search for it, and at last the tenor and I ran across it in a back alley. The driver

BELOW THE HERONRY (Right Branch)

was inside very drunk, and his legs were wedged tight across the cab and no persuasion could move him. The tenor hit him under the knees and he crumpled up for the moment, and before he could get set again, I hustled him out and we laid him gently in the road. I then got on the box and drove the rest of the party back to Stoke. I left the cab outside the front door of the hotel, and I have never heard of it since.

They generally had the best of it. I was once driving up Park Lane in a four-wheeler in a dense fog and was suddenly brought up short, and was embarrassed to find the pole of an omnibus appear under my elbow. It had bored through the back of the cab and missed my spine by inches. On another occasion in a fog in Gower Street a cab " runner " climbed up the back of the four-wheeler and took my kit-bag off the top and vanished into the Ewigkeit. It was so well done that I almost admired him. I had seen him running by the cab and had been pitying him for the disappointment he would have when I turned into Euston.

An even better trick of that sort was once played on me when I was singing at a concert at the old Exeter Hall. A man turned up at about nine o'clock at my house in Kensington Square, and told my servant that there had been a fire at Exeter Hall. My great-coat had been damaged by water and I had sent him for another one. He gave a most vivid account of the scene and the presence of mind of the performers, who had sung calmly on on the platform while the audience passed out in order. He got the great-coat as a just reward for his histrionic powers, but my servant's face when I turned up spick and span in the original one was the only amusing thing at the moment.

From long and bitter experience I was prepared for

bad weather, and when at last I was able to venture forth I fished in a Burberry suit, and never went out without a mackintosh as well. It would take a cloud-burst to get through that combination, so that except for my comfortable habit of falling into the river which has dogged me persistently all my life, I managed to keep fairly dry. But all the clothes in the world could not keep out the Test valley wind. There is, of course, a wind up every valley, and the prevailing wind in the South of England is supposed to be S.W., but at Hurstbourne it was nearly always down the valley, in one's teeth, and N.E., and I could not get it off to Torquay as a regular habit, because it was doing all it wanted on the spot. However, the double mackintosh must have worked the miracle, for at the end of June a tremendous heat-wave came along and a drought which lasted for two months, and from the 12th of July till the 4th of August I never even tried to throw a fly; it was not worth while. It was the hottest weather I have ever known since I was a student in Germany.

One day remains in my mind. I think it was the 9th of August. The heat was terrific. I had to meet my small son at Salisbury Station and get my hair cut in the town. I had first to bicycle 1½ miles to Hurst-bourne. When I got to Salisbury I staggered down into the town to the hairdresser's, and crawled back to the station like a hunted fox on his last legs. When the son in question arrived he insisted on my taking him back into the town to get an ice !

XII

LIFE AT HURSTBOURNE PRIORS

IN most of my spare time during the summer of 1911 I either played cricket or hunted wasps. We had two cricket clubs—the Hurstbourne Priors Club, which played the inter-village League matches, and the Hurstbourne Park Club, which took in members from all round the neighbourhood. As our one object in the latter club was to get good games against really good teams, we used to absorb any good cricketer who came handy and willing as honorary, or temporary, members—such people as F. G. J. Ford, G. Bromley-Martin, Fred Browning, and the like. We played Marlborough (and actually beat them one year), Basingstoke, Highclere and many others, all good cricket and sporting matches. I have vivid recollections of fielding third man at the top of the hill at Marlborough while Shaw (later the Oxford wicket-keeper) was batting. He had a magnificent late cut which he never missed, and which never went in the same place, and I spent a long exhausting afternoon chasing the ball down the hill most of the way to the College. I had an intense admiration for Shaw, for he stood (in spectacles) right up to the wicket to Woodroffe, who was the fastest public-school bowler I have ever seen. Both, alas ! were killed in the war.

But the match we liked best was the one against the Artists, a team brought down each year by Henry Ford. It was a two-day affair, and we used to put up the players in the various houses in the village. It was always a close thing, and each side had complete liberty to co-opt any " swell " they could get hold of. If it could have been proved that W. G. Grace had ever drawn a pig with his eyes shut he would have been accepted as an artist *nem. con.*, and the fact of having been fined for scorching down Hurstbourne hill (a large source of revenue to the county at one time) would have provided, *ipso facto*, sufficient residential qualification for F. S. Jackson to become a Hurst-bourne-Park-er.

We brought off a most successful score against Henry Ford in one of these matches. He had turned up with a certain famous cricketer who would have been ignominiously turned down as an engine-driver, inasmuch as he did not know red from green (or a quaver from a semibreve), and thought that the game was as good as won.

We had, however, in the meantime, unbeknown to him, got hold of his brother Francis (F. G. J. of inter-national fame, spoken of above). We timed his arrival to a nicety. He hovered about the suburbs of Hurst-bourne in a motor-car until we signalled to him that Henry and his team had started for the field, and we stealthily manœuvred him up to the ground at the crucial moment. Henry had won the toss and was sitting in the scoring-box of the pavilion writing out the order of batting. Francis crawled up under the box on his hands and knees with a rug over his head and rose slowly to his feet. Henry gazed fascinated at the giant apparition (Francis is about six feet five), and inch by inch Francis raised the rug, and when the familiar features emerged from cover, there burst forth such a torrent of profanity from Henry as was unusual even among brothers, and we left them to themselves.

We used also to play St. Thomas's Hospital. This was one of the matches we liked best, for they were a very strong lot (A. F. Morcom amongst others) and a delightful set of men. They beat us more often than we beat them.

Even without outside help we could always get a good team, and we were particularly lucky in always having Wyld, who was one of the best amateur wicket-keepers in the country (he was famous in the army cricket of his day ; I hardly ever saw him let a bye), and was always sure of making runs. He was the most persistent " grouser " ever known, and enjoyed himself more thoroughly than anyone in England. Nobody took the smallest notice ; we used just to bide our time and get back on him. Casual visitors looked upon us as very unsympathetic, and tried to convey this to him as politely as they could, but they could never quite make out how it was that there never was a fish in the river, and yet he used to turn up with four brace each evening, and that although there was not a partridge left in the whole of Hampshire, yet he never fired off less than 300 cartridges a day, and very few of them in vain. He was one of the best shots in England. He cursed us one and all at every opportunity, especially his dogs. They appreciated the joke just as much as we did, and used to look at him with adoring eyes and wag their tails hard and roar with laughter.

He had a famous Labrador retriever called " Pilot," whom our children positively worshipped, an affection which was entirely reciprocated by him. His imaginary exploits as a poacher were a god-send to me as a pre-bed *raconteur*. They were atrocious libels, for he was morally *sans peur et sans reproche*, and his manners and his prowess as a retriever were proverbial all over the county. Nobody got more roundly abused than he, and no one enjoyed it more. He was a genius at picking up after a drive and kept every bird in his memory till the beat was over ; no runner had a chance with him.

He knew the game from A to Z, and practically never transgressed under any stress of excitement. But there was one brilliant exception. Wyld was shooting at Bradwell Grove in Oxfordshire, and it had been agreed that there was to be no shooting between beats. This Pilot thoroughly approved of. As they were moving from one stand to another a rabbit got up, and one of the guns in a moment of forgetfulness let fly at it and missed. It went down wide past the others and they all had a shot at it, strictly against orders. Every soul missed it, and it bolted into the covert. It was too much for Pilot. If one rule was broken, why not another ? He dashed after it. " Leave him alone ! " shouted the host (who knew him well), " he'll bring back something." He was quite right. Pilot turned up in ten minutes with a hare !

There was one other time when Pilot was diverted from the path of orthodoxy. Wilkinson had taken a small shoot at Stoke, a high tableland near Hurstbourne Tarrant. We went off there one day in early January to try to pick up an odd bird or two, and we borrowed Pilot for the occasion. The party consisted of Wilkinson, Monypenny, the gardener and myself, and we went in an open car. It was the coldest day I ever remember in England, which is saying a good deal. Pilot started off in a fever of excitement, hustling us off the cushions so that he could get a good view. In five minutes he was on the floor huddled against our legs for warmth. The cold was so intense that an hour of trying to walk against the north-easter was

enough for us, and we determined to go home, but
the gardener, with the spirit of the ancient martyrs,
volunteered to take Pilot and drive the birds to us
while we lined the hedges. I would give a good deal
to have a photograph of that line. I was standing with
my gun under my arm and both hands in my pockets
with one eye emerging from my coat-collar and peering
through the hedge. I was suffering untold tortures
myself, and I thought I would have a look and see how
the others were standing it. Wilkinson was apparently
in a state of coma with his head huddled on his chest.
Monypenny was lying in the ditch. Their guns were
on the ground and their backs were towards the birds.
Pilot was not a conspicuous success as a beater, as
Wilkinson's game-book shows :

Stoke, Jan. 6. Blizzard. One pigeon.

He was as near human as any dog could be, and his
appreciation of his master's affection for him was a
delight to see. He knew he was the apple of his eye
in reality, and the more red-hot the imprecations the
more broadly he grinned and the faster his tail wagged.
He was the true big-dog of the fairy tale, beloved of
children and small dogs alike. My small son once gave
him a lump of sugar. He had no sooner given it than
he repented of it, and I saw him, to my horror, suddenly put a fat arm half-way down Pilot's throat,
retrieve the sugar, and put it back in his own mouth
and swallow it before I could do a thing.

Wyld looked upon all the visiting rods as criminals
(or pretended to) and swore that each and all of them
completely " skinned " the river. He was prepared to
take his oath that one particular pirate used to arrive
by motor at 5.30 a.m. every day, and pulled his last
fish out by lamplight under the Beehive Bridge,

somewhere about midnight. The poor man was a perfectly normal member of society, but unfortunately for him he had first come under observation at an inauspicious moment.

Wyld was playing cricket one day up in the park, and had hit the ball far out into the country. He was running jubilantly between the wickets, when he was surprised to feel the ball, which he imagined was half-way to Whitchurch, hit him a terrific blow on the back of the leg, and over he went like a shot rabbit. As a matter of fact, he had broken his " Kangaroo " tendon. This incapacitated him for some time, and he used to spend his afternoons with his leg on a chair, and a pair of field glasses in his hand, watching the river and wondering what Billy and Pom Pom and Hannibal and Slippery Sam were doing at the moment at the top of their weed-beds. One day the unfortunate individual referred to above drifted into his field of vision. I was there at the time and I never want a better entertainment than I got listening to Wyld's infuriated ejaculations as the sportsman spotted, and began to stalk, each of his old friends in turn. We both knew them far better than he did, and our triumphant delight as he rose each time from his knees, baffled, mingled with Wyld's indignation that he was ever allowed on the water or had ever been born at all, helped to make it one of the best " movie " shows I ever saw.

Wyld was a very difficult person to score off, as he was as clever as a fox, but we did it once. He and I had been invited to dinner and bridge by Wilkinson and Monypenny. He was very pleased with himself on that particular evening, for he had made a lot of runs in the afternoon and he had had a very good dinner, and he approached the card-table in high good

humour with life generally. We had meanwhile
" faked " a particular pack of cards which was to be
produced at the proper psychological moment. When
this moment came we surreptitiously slipped in this
pack in place of the real one, cut and dealt. Monypenny's hand, as arranged, consisted of ace, queen and
eight other clubs, and three small diamonds. He was
on Wyld's left. I was Wyld's partner and had five
small spades, five small hearts and three small diamonds. Wilkinson was Monypenny's partner and
was, of course, on Wyld's right. He had ace, ten,
nine and eight of diamonds, knave, ten, four and
three of spades, knave, ten, nine, seven of hearts
and one club. Wyld had king, queen, knave of
diamonds, ace, king, queen and eight of spades, ace
king, queen and two of hearts, and king, knave of
clubs. It must be remembered that we three were all
conspirators and that declarations and passes were
made to programme. I have purposely described the
hands in advance.

It was Wyld's deal and Wilkinson cut the cards in
an innocent manner. Wyld dealt and went one no-
trump. Monypenny went two clubs and I passed.
Wilkinson went two diamonds. Wyld with a " poker "
face went two no-trumps. We did not dare to risk
another rise so Monypenny doubled at once. Wyld
gave a jump, thought for a long time whether he would
re-double but finally said " No." Monypenny led a
diamond. Wilkinson took it with the ace, and led his
single club through the king, knave. Monypenny
promptly ran off ten clubs on end.

I shall never forget the *difficilis descensus* of that
hand or the *crescendo* of Wyld's language during his
discard as all his winning cards were dragged from
him like teeth. All his kings and queens and knaves

of hearts and spades and diamonds were shed from his hand, each with a groan and a curse, until he was left with the two aces—spades and hearts. Monypenny led one of his small diamonds and then the fun really began. Wyld had long ago forgotten all about the diamonds and would naturally have supposed that if anybody had them it would be the man who had declared them. He surpassed all our expectations when it came to the choice of the two aces. Finally he tossed up a coin, heads for spades and tails for hearts. It came down a head, and he threw the heart and Monypenny led the last diamond and won a grand slam.

It was a success far beyond our dreams. Wyld sat there for about a quarter of an hour, going over the game again and again, scratching his head and declaiming against fate, getting us to reassemble the hands, so that he could send the whole thing to the *Field*, while Wilkinson and Monypenny commiserated with him, and I, his partner, took each of his ancestors in turn and said what I thought of them and their present-day product. He was exactly like a dog who has fallen out of the window, half of the people patting him on the head and rubbing his back and saying, " Poor old chap ! " and the other half telling him what a fool he was to fall asleep upon the window-sill. And while he was still dazed with the outrage of the whole thing we dealt round a pack of " Happy Family," and when he picked up his hand he found that he had thirteen representatives of Mr. Bones the Butcher and Miss Bung the Brewer's daughter.

Savage and Sharkey were like Orestes and Pylades. Their friendship was one of the most happy things I have ever seen, and it was all the more happy in that it was not demonstratively visible on the surface. Very much the reverse. Their language about one another—especially Savage's about Sharkey—bore a resemblance to Wyld's to Pilot. It was after a golf-match that one heard Savage at his best. He was not much of a player and, no matter what the handicap was, he invariably lost. Sharkey had a leisurely style of play which always " got there." It drove Savage wild, and you would see him stalking off the last green by himself, his eyes blazing red through his spectacles, spluttering out incandescent descriptions of Sharkey and all his ways.

A friend of Savage's once said to me that he did not know which was the most conspicuous thing about him—his genius, his courage, or his integrity. I could not think of a better description of him so far as it goes, but I should like to add two more to the list of his virtues—his vibrant vitality and his blessed sense of humour.

He was, as everyone knows, the greatest alienist of his day, and it was deeply interesting to hear him talk on this subject and on his experiences. He was a famous climber, and would have been President of the Alpine Club had it not been for his deafness. He told me the story of how this deafness came about. He was inter-viewing a patient at an asylum. He knew that she was dangerous and he was watching her quietly, when suddenly she hit him a terrific blow with her left hand on his right ear, smashing the drum. She was left-handed and he had been carefully watching her right arm.

He was also a high authority as a botanist, and his garden in the summer was a joy to behold. I always turned in there for tea when I was fishing anywhere near, whether they were there or not ; we were all one happy family.

He knew nothing about music, but played the

pianola vigorously—as Sharkey discovered later chiefly as a form of exercise ! He went to concerts and even to the opera. We went together once to *Parsifal*. He slept through most of the first act. He woke up during the Amfortas music and whispered to me :

" Have I been asleep ? "

" Yes," I said.

" Good Heavens ! " he said, " When did I go off ? Was it the swan ? "

It was the swan.

He had a dog-like devotion for Sharkey, and though he growled and swore at him he was touchingly dependent on him. Sharkey, besides being a first-rate fisherman and a very good golfer, was just as famous in his own line as Savage was in his, and, as the latter's medical adviser, had a bad time. If the treatment did not happen to fit in with the patient's inclinations, no attention was paid to it.

Savage loved company. He either went out to a dinner-party or had one of his own every night of his life. The results were obvious. About once a month he would be completely knocked out by gout and indigestion. Then Sharkey would be called in. He would tell him plainly what a fool he had been and would threaten to wash his hands of him once and for all, and would finally prescribe for him. Savage would agree humbly, and would dine out again the first night he was able to get about.

Sharkey told me of one particular instance, which, he said, might be taken as an example of all of them. Savage had been really bad—worse than usual—and he had talked to him most seriously. He had put him on the strictest diet and forbidden him, under pain of awful possibilities, to dine outside of his own house until further notice. Savage had meekly admitted the

justice of the criticism and the propriety of the treatment, and butter would not have melted in his mouth.

A month later they were fishing together at Hurstbourne. They had agreed to meet for luncheon at a
certain spot on the Tufton water. When Sharkey
arrived at the tryst he could see no sign of Savage, so
he sat down to wait for him. Presently he became
aware of a dilapidated figure sitting on a hurdle with
its head in its hands. He went over to it and said :

" Hullo ! Savage, what's up ? "

There came a long sepulchral groan from Savage.

" Sharkey," he said, " my stomach's in rags ! "

Sharkey thought for a moment, and then he said :

" Look here, Savage, tell me the truth. How long is
it since you dined at home ? "

There was a long—a very long—pause and then a
far-away voice murmured :

" Three weeks."

He was delighted with this story himself when he
saw it afterwards in perspective, as he invariably was
with any joke that was " on him." The famous
" Savage " Christmas cards, drawn by his friend
Arthur Rackham, were variants of his fishing exploits,
so humorous at his expense that they were actually
disapproved of by one or two purists who could not
reconcile his greatness with flippancy.

One of these Christmas cards came in handy to me.
He and Sharkey used to swear that I poached all the
trout out of the river, and I used to commiserate with
them at not having learned their elementary technique
early enough in life to be really good. I would point to
the " fly-refuser," as a very good fish to learn casting
from, and would pointedly open my bag and pretend to
choose one trout out of four brace and offer it to them
for breakfast next morning. One day I happened to

I

break my rod just opposite their cottage, so I went in to borrow one of theirs. There were half a dozen of them lying along the pegs in the hall. I chose the one I liked best and fairly chuckled when I found that it had a salmon-fly all ready set up on it. My enemy was delivered into my hand. There were various explanations. It had been brought down from Scotland in that form and they had forgotten to take it down ; but after profuse expressions of admiration at their powers of muscular endurance while holding the rod outside the window for some ten hours on end, and sarcastic inquiries as to how the passengers in the other compartments had dodged it when they got in and out, and what the policeman at Piccadilly Circus had said when it tickled the back of his head in the " hold-up," they abandoned that tack and said that they kept it there as a permanent testimony to the crudity of salmon-fishing as compared with the ooo dun. It was, no doubt, one of the weapons of attack on the " fly-refuser " and in that capacity earned my secret respect and admiration.

The last, alas ! of the Savage Christmas cards is called : " I chatter, chatter, as I go." In it he and Rackham are depicted starting off from the cottage on a fishing expedition, with their rods in their hands ready for use. By a happy coincidence one of the artist's " twiddles " (part of the foliage of a tree), appeared in the exact place on the rod where the salmon-fly had been—in the form of a long and sinuous worm !

The cottage (built in 1750) had sheltered famous men and fishermen before Savage and Sharkey. Their friend and immediate predecessor, the late Mr. G. H. Haydon, treasurer of Bethlem, was himself a fisherman of renown, and many's the fairy tale I heard of his and

A MERRY · CHRISTMAS
from · the · Savage · Family

" I chatter, chatter, as I go
To join the brimming river "

the Bourne's partnership. He was closely associated
with various members of the staff of *Punch*, and was a
particular friend of John Leech. The latter often stayed
with him at the cottage and made some of the famous
fishing drawings actually on the spot. Who knows
but that Mr. Briggs' immortal pike which sprang at
him and barked like a dog may have been the immediate predecessor of the fly-refuser !

XIII

THE fishing this season was a varied experience—Chilbolton, Bransbury, Mottisfont, Midleton and Blagdon. I remember the Chilbolton days better than any, for I had one or two triumphs and one or two humiliations there, and one evening's journey home which is indelibly fixed in my mind, as it was one of the rare occasions in my life when I have been absolutely exhausted physically. It lasted less than an hour, but it made up for it in other ways.

I had gone by train to Wherwell in my salmon-waders and had brought a bicycle with me, as there was no late train back. I had had a worse day than usual as far as the " going " was concerned, being most of the time half-way up to my waist in mud and having to drag each leg out by main force. It was pitch dark when I started home and I had had nothing to eat since luncheon. I had a heavy basket of fish to carry as well as the rest of my tackle, and, to finish up with, my rod jammed at the joints and I could not take it down. There was nothing for it but to tie it on to the bicycle with about six feet of it sticking out in front, in imminent danger of being snapped off in a hedge if I veered a foot from the straight line. If you have ever got on to a bicycle in salmon-waders, you will know that you do not get off again in a hurry, for it is the most perilous ascent imaginable and is generally followed by a series of drunken gyrations all over the road before you get your balance, especially if, as I do, you hate bicycles like poison. If, in addition to all this, you have your favourite rod sticking out far ahead of you, and fanning the air up and down and from side to side, your every impulse is to steer straight into the ditch and smash it and the bicycle and yourself into smithereens.

That journey was a nightmare. It is about seven miles from Chilbolton to Hurstbourne and for a full half of the way it is a veritable switchback. I can still feel the weight of those leaden waders and see the point of that rod switching up and down, dashing into the bushes on one side of the road and across to the other in sympathy with the agonising skids of the bicycle, lashing the ground in the feeble lamplight and springing back again. It certainly had a good joke at my expense, but I did not appreciate it. I fell into bed the moment I got in, being long past food.

The first of the triumphs I spoke of was followed immediately by its humiliation. There was a particular three-pounder which lay in mid-stream a couple of hundred yards below the Winchester road. I knew him well, and so apparently did other people. There was a regular passage through the flags at the only possible place of approach, where each of his enemies had hoped that he himself was going to be the one exception to the rule. I was one of them. I walked boldly into it the first time, only to see him fade gently out of sight. I tried him several times from the same place on that and subsequent occasions, always with the same result. No matter how greedily he was feeding, the moment the top of my head or my rod appeared in the opening he slowly sank. So one day, realising what a fool I had been, I lit a pipe and sat down to think it out, and suddenly the solution came to me. What was the good of

standing six feet four in my boots, if I was not going
to take advantage of it ? I crawled up to the bank
below him and got into the water. I could not see the
bottom and did not know how far down it was or what
it was made of, but I slid in on chance. It came up to
the very top of my salmon-waders, and I never stole
so gingerly on the tips of my toes since the days when
I used to rob the larder as a small boy in Ireland. Fortunately there was a pollard on my left and I hung on
to this as I threw the line. He was quite unsuspicious.
His danger-point was that passage in the flags. So
long as he watched that he was safe, and the Irish
giant to the best of his belief was reposing in the Hun-
terian Museum at the Royal College of Surgeons. So
when my fly arrived with the others he sucked it in
happily. He dashed off up-stream and in a moment my
waders were full of water, but I was so hilarious with
triumph that I did not care. I played him up and down
for about five minutes and then the fly came away.
I never saw him again on that day or any other, and I
did not very much mind : in the battle of wits I had
come out the winner, and that was what I chiefly
wanted.

But he meant having his revenge and he arranged a
little surprise for me. When I had emptied my waders
and put them on again—the most vile sensation in the
world—I strolled on up the bank, and as I came round
a corner by some pollards I saw another fine fish rising.
All I had to do was to get down the bank at the turn,
where I should be hidden by the trees, and out into the
water which seemed comparatively shallow just here.
Down I went in every sense of the word. At the first
step I took I sank above my waist into a deep bog of
black mud. I had not a moment to think ; I was slip-
ping rapidly out of sight in a filthy quick-sand. Over

into the water went my rod with a splash (and off went the fish). I made a despairing grab in the air with my right hand, and by extreme good luck just managed to catch hold of the root of a tree. It took me a full quarter of an hour to work myself out of the poisonous-smelling slough of despond, covered with slime, wet to the skin and, worst of all, humiliated, for I firmly believe it was a put-up job by my friend down below.

Savage and Sharkey were once scored off in very much the same way by the " fly-refuser." They had, as they thought, exhausted all the ways of approach, until it occurred to Savage that they might stalk him from the rickety punt which lay at the steps of their bathing-place. He ordered Sharkey aboard and Sharkey meekly went and meekly held the two rods while Savage shoved off.

The punt, being an old friend of the fly-refuser, immediately collapsed. Savage said afterwards that when he came up all he saw was two rods sticking out of the water with two hands underneath them and that the rest of Sharkey did not turn up for about five minutes.

There was another fish which put Savage on his back. I was delighted, because he had a few days before, in the course of an argument, put me on my back by an underhand bit of elementary ju-jitsu. This fish had been hooked in the saw-mill shallows and had run straight back through Savage's legs. In a moment the whole three, fish, rod and man, were in an inextricable tangle and Savage was on his back in the water, grabbing at the fish like a demon. He got him in the end, and I think he was prouder of that catch than any he ever made.

He was not a really expert fisherman and the story of his first success was a remarkable one. His period

of adolescence was very long, and it was actually two
years before he ever landed a fish at all ! Then one
day he turned up with five beautiful trout. The others
were petrified with astonishment, but to all their
suggestions of gunpowder and nets and the like he
replied that he had caught them on a dry-fly. He told
them, eventually, that he had been fishing as usual
without any success, in spite of the fact that there was a
heavy rise. There had been a high wind and leaves
were floating down thick on the water. He noticed
presently that the fish seemed to be rising at the leaves
themselves. He watched carefully and saw that they
were actually taking some fly or grub off the edge of
the leaf as it came down. He picked up a leaf, stuck
his fly into the edge of it, and cast it upon the waters
and promptly hooked and killed the five he had
brought home.

There is a certain hole in the Hurstbourne Park golf
course known as " The Chasm," a name which describes it accurately. You have to drive across a yawning valley, and if you pitch short, as you generally do,
your ball hits the far bank and trickles undulatingly
into a rabbit hole. Sharkey and Savage were playing
across the Chasm, and Savage's ball had duly made its
way into " Chatsworth," otherwise rabbit-hole No.
X15 on the map. They groped and dug for it in vain ;
nothing but a vacuum cleaner could have brought it
out of its abysmal depths ; so they continued the
round, and in due course came to the Chasm once
more. There was Savage's ball perched up outside the
hole like an ornament on a wedding cake ! It had evidently circulated into the middle of the rabbit family,
and paterfamilias had said, " Let's kick the beastly
thing out," and no sooner said than done.

I am certain that trout—some of them at any rate—

have an organised system of defence. Every fisherman knows the maddening swarm of little fish that tear up-stream ahead of him to warn the big one that the enemy is approaching. I have seen the same big fellow in the same place day after day with the same body of scouts in the same station, and have stalked him with the same futile results. There was one in particular just above the bridge at the bottom of the Park stream at Stock-bridge, which provided me with a brilliant demonstration of the system. He lay below a patch of weeds under the near bank and he had a series of squads of retainers in echelon, who passed the news up to him group by group. He would feed placidly until the final bunch began to fidget and then he would slowly wag his tail and glide under cover. He is probably there still and deserves to be.

I had, however, on a subsequent day at Chilbolton another triumph which in the *à propos* arrival of the right man at the right moment was comparable to the goal which one dropped in dreams at school when one's house was *in extremis*. I had been fishing the lower water all the morning and was to meet the Patricks at luncheon at Butcher's Mead by the bridge on the Winchester Road. They had some people stay-ing with them who had never seen a dry-fly in their lives. These were rather sceptical and humorous on the subject, as we picknicked in the meadow by the river.

I had had a miserable day, absolutely blank, and had not seen a rise since I started. I had been watching the river casually all through lunch and had seen noth-ing stir, but just as I lit my pipe I saw a good fish rise in the middle about thirty yards up, and at that very moment one of the strangers, quite unaware of this, said chaffingly, " Now let's see you catch one of those famous dry-fly fish we've heard such a lot about."

I yawned as far as was consistent with good manners and said, " All right ! " I got up very slowly, stretched prodigiously, shook myself a bit, got my rod and net with an air of profound boredom, sauntered down the bank and waded out into mid-stream and cast over the spot where he had risen. The light on the water was perfect and the little iron-blue stood out beautifully for those on the bank to see. Up he came at once and off he went with the reel showing off for the occasion. He played his part nobly, for he fought far above his weight of 1¼ lbs., and raced up and down, leaping high into the air at the end of every other rush, to the intense excitement of the party on shore ; and when at last I landed him and handed him over to the scoffer I was looked upon as Solomon was by the Queen of Sheba. The half had not been told her. It was one of those rare instances where good luck set the stage complete.

The best score of this sort that I ever heard of was made by the late Mr. William Le Fanu (brother of Joseph Sheridan Le Fanu of *Uncle Silas* fame, and himself the writer of one of the best books of reminiscences in the world—*Seventy Years of Irish Life*). He and my father used to fish the little Dargle river close to their respective homes near Enniskerry in Co. Wicklow. It was a dark little mountain burn which got bigger as it neared the sea at Bray, and like all such small streams that come from the peat it was full of little trout. But like many of them it also held one or two monsters in certain deep holes. Mr. Le Fanu knew them all, and had often tried for them in vain, but on this particular occasion he had got one of them (presumably on a worm), and it weighed five pounds ! It was at a point where the Bray road runs right alongside the river. He threw him into the grass by his side, and began setting up a cast of small flies. Just then a man came by on the road and stopped and leaned on the wall. He was a member of what in Ireland is graphically described as the " Spit Club," and proved himself an able exponent of its objects while he smoked. He looked on in silence for a long time, chuckling to himself, and at last he laughed outright and said :

" Ah ! what's the use of your wastin' your time ? There's nothin' but wee little things in it."

" Indeed, that's true for you," said Mr. Le Fanu. Here he bent down and slowly lifted up the five-pounder. " We've nothing bigger than this."

He was luckier than I once was under somewhat similar circumstances in Germany. It was at Bayreuth, and Hermann Levi, the famous conductor of *Parsifal*, had heard me talking about fishing and had professed a desire to see how it was done ; so I arranged with him to take him to Rupprechtstegen (some little way by train from Bayreuth), where there was a capital trout-stream which I knew well. It was a bad day and I never saw a fish rise. I knew nothing about " minor tactics " in those days and, in a feverish anxiety to make good, I kept throwing a dry March-brown, or something similar, into likely places. After an hour of watching me crawling about dripping with perspiration and not even the sign of an " anbeissen," Levi suddenly threw his arms into the air and said : " Und das nennt man wahrhaftig ein Vergnügen ! " (" And that's what they call pleasure ! "), and walked off slowly to the station.

I had one other spectacular triumph—not at Chilbolton this time—for which again the stage was set complete and everything came off.

I was fishing the evening rise just above the bridge at Stockbridge, and the bridge itself was lined with

Tommies and American flying-men from the aviation ground in the neighbourhood. I was trying for a rising fish just off the little carrier on the left, and he was treating me with bored indifference. He was taking flies all round him but languidly leaving me out whenever I came along, and I could hear the amused *crescendo* of comments from the crowd behind me, indicating a decided preference for the brain-power of the fish to that of the fisherman. Here I suppose is where one's training as a public performer comes in. Not only did I determine that I was going to capture that fish and the audience with him, but I *knew* that I was going to get him and I meant to get him as dramatically as possible. I took off my orange-quill (generally the most deadly fly at Stockbridge at that hour) amid the delighted good-humoured sarcasms of the crowd, and put up my old friend iron-blue. That did it. He took it at once. He not only took it but he leapt about three feet into the air and fell back on to the water with a crack like a pistol-shot, and rushed off upstream with the reel yelling. But the Tommies on the bridge yelled louder. They suddenly became my bosom friends and admirers and shouted advice and encouragement from above my head. There were several moments when I could have brought him into the net, but I meant to spin out the excitement, so I let him go off on his travels wherever he liked and once even eased him off right under the bridge where they could see him under their noses, a move which was very popular. I finally landed him down there (he was 2 lbs.), and when I had knocked him on the head I held him up and said, " Who'll have him ? " and threw him up on to the bridge, and then I saw one of the finest scrummages of my life ; and in the middle of it, to liven matters up, a motor-lorry dashed through them at top speed, scattering them right and left. How it was they were not all killed I do not know. I only know that whenever I think of that fish I feel a certain glow of satisfaction at the success of the one and only time in my life when I deliberately played to the gallery.

Not quite the only time, now I come to think of it. My brother and I did it in a disgraceful way at Stuttgart. When we introduced lawn-tennis in the skating-rink there we made it almost a fine art. He and I were the only exponents of the game at first, and the play consisted of singles between us two. At a given signal we would abandon the idea of contest altogether and go in for a species of pat-ball, keeping up the rallies as long as we could and trying hard not to laugh. It was an infantile form of sport, but it served its purpose, for it was invariably accompanied by choked screams and clutchings and tumultuous applause from the audience. When I look back on it now I try to persuade myself that it was a purely proselytising manœuvre, an attempt to convert our neighbours to the English game, the end justifying the means.

The singer is supposed to swallow flattery wholesale without turning a hair. It was once too much for me. It was in the spring of 1893, when I was in America, and I had been invited to the opening of a new fishing club in Long Island. It was pond-like and virgin water, and the trout thought the millennium had arrived. We paddled about in boats and in the course of one miserable hour I got my limit. Next evening I was at a party in New York and heard my hostess mention my name. She began with some complimentary remarks about my singing at the Symphony Concerts, which I took in my stride ; but when she went on to say, " and he fishes like a dream ! " I thought of Wildbad and blushed for shame.

There is a certain hidden delight in " showing off "
which is deeply rooted in all living things. It is the
motive power which convinces the flapper that she
was born to be a cinema star and makes the dog cross
his paws on his chest and tell you that he is a knight
who has died for his country. It is linked up with
personality and attraction, the power to hold the eyes
and ears of other men, the greatest gift in the world—
what is commonly called " Magnetism." But true
magnetism and playing to the gallery, though they
may have had a common ancestor, are as far as the
poles apart in the ethics of performance. The one is
unconscious, compelling and incomparably precious,
the other studied, opportunistic, cheap and nasty. I
remember years ago at a theatrical dinner hearing
Fernandez, a well-known actor of the old school,
recite, " Over the hills to the poorhouse." If ever there
was an old war-horse it is that particular poem. I suppose every member of his audience had heard it, or
recited it himself, hundreds of times. Yet the men on
either side of me were crying. That was personality,
utterly unconscious of its own mechanism, yet over-
whelming in its power. And I have heard a singer of
world-wide reputation when singing Brahms's " Ver-
gebliches Ständchen," a little humorous serenade sung
sotto voce throughout and finishing in a whisper, make a
long pause before the penultimate note, take a deep
breath, leap to the octave above and hold it *fortissimo*
to the end !

The singer's duty in the scheme of things is a simple
one. He is a messenger and nothing else. He has to
take a message from the poet and the composer and
give it to the world at large. He is chosen for this
duty as being the best man available for the purpose.
If he plays to the gallery he calls attention to himself

instead of to the message. That is a dereliction of duty. If he has personality as well, his crime is the greater.

This applies equally to all the arts and, indeed, to all the games. The very rules are the same, whether they be technical or moral. It is a curious thing, but true, that the main rules of the singer's technique are " Keep your eye on the word," " Don't press," and " Follow through ! "

XIV

BLAGDON

THE year 1911 was a remarkable one. During the months of June and July not a fly ever appeared on the water, and fishing was a dead-letter. But at least, as I said before, it was warm—with a vengeance—though to make up for it the wind was east the whole time, and east wind arouses every criminal instinct in my being. I spent most of my time hunting wasps.

I went to Blagdon in September with Sir Desmond O'Callaghan and H. T. Sheringham. It was the usual east wind hopeless weather, but I remember the trip chiefly from the fact that I slipped the sheath of a nerve or muscle (whichever it is), in my shoulder the very first day, and had my left arm crippled for the rest of the visit. It was a most uncalled-for and painful insult, for I was sitting quietly on a bank having luncheon, when someone apparently ran a red-hot skewer through my shoulder. Both my companions were quite capable of doing it in view of the East wind, but they were not close enough and I could not saddle them with it. A friend of mine told me that he once ran over a dog in Cirencester, and when he pulled up to pick up the remains he was astounded to see the dog pick himself up, rush across the street and seize another dog by the scruff of the neck and shake him like a rat. Those were my sensations on this occasion.

There were no very big fish this year, but I lost two

splendid ones in Mr. Griffith's water at Kimbridge entirely through my own fault. I forgot to put up a fresh cast for the big water and both broke me in the open.

There was one, however, which gave me one of the most interesting fights I ever had. It was on the upper beat of Midleton. He lay at the bottom of an island where a carrier joins the main-stream and the food from both was carried down to him. There was a barbed wire cattle-fence from the end of the island to the near bank farther down, and he lay with his tail against one of the posts. He had a little kingdom of his own within this ring-fence, and he was a real pleasure to watch as he shone against the golden gravel, short and thick, with shoulders like a bull and spotted like a leopard. There was a big tree which smothered me at the ordinary casting-distance, and the only way I could get at him was by kneeling in a bunch of tall flags quite close up to him and throwing a very short line, peering through the flags to see where my fly fell. He paid all sorts of visits to it, making my heart jump, but spurning it each time, before I finally got him off his guard ; but the really interesting part came after he was hooked, for I had to play him by watching the point of my rod and the direction of the line. I was so close to him that if I had shown my head over the top of the flags he would have dashed out under the barbed wire into the main stream and broken me to pieces. He did make several excursions in that direction, but he always came back to his beat, and I finally wore him out by making him swim against the steady pull. He made one or two rushes to try to rid himself of the encumbrance, but most of the time he swam straight up and down the barbed wire enclosure. What made it so interesting to me was the fact that

K

from the moment I hooked him until I got him into the net ten minutes or so later, I never once caught a fair view of him. He was the prettiest 2½-pounder I ever saw.

1912

I only fished seven times in 1912, and got twenty-one fish weighing 37 lbs. Six of these I caught at Blagdon (of which more presently). But one day in July I had a convincing proof of the powers of the iron-blue. It was on the Longparish House water on the Test, and I had been trying half the morning for two fish which were lying beside one another in mid-stream.

I had experimented alternately with olives, and gingers, and hare's ears and others, but though they were rising freely I could never get them to come. When I put up the iron-blue, I got the two fish in two casts. I had not had any intention when I started of making exhaustive experiments or of weeding out the various patterns, but as I went on I determined to reserve my little friend to the end, and see if it really was demonstrably so superior to all the rest, and it left me without any doubt, if I had ever had any.

I was pursued by gales every time I went out, and spent most of another day on the same water hiding from the squalls. There was a tremendous rise of duns that day, but it was next to impossible to get a fly on the water, or see it when it got there. I find, however, that I killed one of 1¾ lbs., which was a " perfect specimen of the old Test trout."

The old Test trout seems to be rapidly disappearing from the upper waters of that river. He is being ousted, or outbred, by a certain yellow-bellied variety which was unfortunately introduced about fifteen years ago.

This fish is more like the Kennet trout in shape, long and thin and dark, as opposed to the real Test fish, who is short and thick and silvery ; but the resemblance ceases with the shape, for he is sluggish and puts up a poor fight ; the most that can be said for him is that he is fairly good to eat. I was fishing in the summer of 1923 for a few days on the Bourne, and felt sadder than ever, for every fish I killed was a yellow-bellied apology ; I did not see a single specimen of the old Test trout in or out of the water.

At the end of August O'Callaghan and Sheringham and I went to Blagdon again. We were only there for two days, but I got six fish weighing $17\frac{1}{2}$ lbs. Two of them ($3\frac{1}{4}$ and $3\frac{3}{4}$) are firmly fixed in my mind. The first took the whole of my line and most of the backing in his first rush. He simply disappeared under water, and I had nothing to do except stand there and see the line rush out. He stopped at last just as the metal was beginning to show through the backing. Presently I saw a big trout leap high out of the water far out in the lake, and I said to Sheringham, who was standing beside me, " I'd like to be into that one," and then he leaped again and it suddenly dawned on me that this was my own fish, and I was into him after all. I never saw a fish jump out of the water so consistently as he did all the way in. He was foul-hooked in the stomach.

The second was the one I referred to in the introduction as having been an embarrassment to me, and which I positively resented having on my line. Incredible but true ! There was an evening rise on, and the big fish were taking the fly on the surface. I was fishing dry, and after a while hooked this particular beauty. At ordinary times he would have been good enough for anybody, but he had hardly started on his wanderings when a huge monster of about 7 or 8 lbs.

rose in front of me within easy casting distance and
sailed slowly up and down head-and-tailing, sucking
the flies down right and left, calm in his sense of perfect
security, knowing as he did that that big dry Wickham
was occupied elsewhere. He must have known it, for
the moment I had landed my 3¾-pounder, he went
down and never appeared again, though the rise
remained on for another half-hour. It was really
tragic; by all the ordinary chances he should have been
mine.

In those days the evening rise was one of the features
of the place. It came on at sundown and lasted from
half an hour to an hour. The actual fly was probably
the big green midge, which in the evening light looked
as big as a March-brown, but it was not in the least
necessary to put it up specially. Any big fly, such as an
orange-quill or Wickham on an o hook, would do.
(Sheringham used a No. 4 Wickham.) If he came across
it he took it. You could concentrate enough thrills
into that evening half-hour of Blagdon to last you a
lifetime. You would see a four-pounder cruising
along within distance, almost silhouetted against the
evening light as his head and tail showed up, and
picking up anything within reach. You had only to
drop a big dry quill in his path, and if he did not turn
aside from his line of direction he took your fly without
fail. He never refused, and, as the water was still, I
just sat there and waited for him. It was a queer
combination of passivity and excitement, unique in its
conditions and stage setting.

The Blagdon brown trout is very like the white
trout in his manners. You could swear that he had
just come up from the sea, for he fights like a sailor,
and is pink as a salmon and about the best fish to eat
that swims. I have hardly ever seen a bad-conditioned

THE BROAD WATER

fish there (except a diseased one up a creek which I managed to snatch and destroy). Both brown and rainbows always seem in the pink of condition, and I will back a Blagdon 1½ lbs. rainbow to win the featherweight championship of the world. I am prepared to back that assertion. I know it from bitter experience.

Colonel Llewellyn (Chief Constable of Wiltshire), Francis Harford and I were fishing together at Blagdon in the summer of 1923. We had been told of a mighty eight-pounder which came in the evening to feed on the flats opposite the hut. As I had to leave on the morning following this particular day, I was sent to have the first try for it. Llewellyn was sceptical and said he preferred to fish a beat of his own, so Harford came with me. We waded out about 200 yards and began fishing in a state of suppressed excitement. Nothing happened for an hour, and then there came a sudden tug at my rod and away the monster (as I thought) went. He seemed absolutely inexhaustible. Not once but many times he took me out to within a yard or two of the end of my backing ; and when, after one of the most exciting fights I ever remember, I finally landed him he was only a 1½ lb. rainbow ! My only consolation—apart from the fight—was the thought that the eight-pounder had thought it advisable to keep out of my way.

He was evidently proportionately contemptuous of Llewellyn, for the next evening when the latter took my place, he positively rushed at him. I understand that he gambolled all round him, nose-diving and looping the loop, finally taking his fly and cast and running off with them. Llewellyn had made no special preparations for him. To begin with, he had not bothered to put on stout tackle so early in the evening and, to go on with, he did not believe that there was

sich a person at all. All that he now remembers is
hearing one long terrified scream from his reel and
seeing a thing like a porpoise plunging off to the far
side of the lake in a series of switchback leaps, with a
long streamer of 3X gut blowing behind him in the
gale.

Alas ! the evening rise seems to have deserted the
lake. Perhaps it, too, like the Bourne, has a hidden
sorrow. There are signs of its re-birth, but for many
years it has been but a memory. But one evening in
September 1918 (I think) it gave us a glimpse of its
old glories. The circumstances here again were
positively uncanny.

Gran Bromley-Martin and I, and Donald Carr, who
is in charge of the whole fishing, had been talking
about the old evening rise and the latter had been
bewailing to us that it was a thing of the past. Nothing
approaching a rise had been seen there, he said, for
several years, and he was unable to account for it
except by the supposition that the surface fly had perished ; and together we shed tears over the days that
were no more.

At sundown that same evening we were standing far
out in the lake, fishing blind. Neither of us had felt a
pull, and we were monotonously pursuing the technique of the wet fly, when without a word of warning
the whole lake went mad with the most wonderful
evening rise I have ever seen. The water that a moment
before had been dead came suddenly to life with a rise
of mighty fish. The glass of the lake all in a moment
was studded thick with flies. They were about the size
of a March-brown and were clearly visible in the
waning light. We could see and hear the fish sucking
them down in a frenzy. They seemed to have gone
crazy at the sight of their old friends. There would be

twenty of them rising at the same time within casting distance. I could have kicked them with my foot as they came up all around me. I do not believe they knew or cared whether we were there or not. I tried them with every dry-fly I could think of. I was just as excited as they were and did not have the sense to pick up one of the flies and see what it was. I thought that, as in former times, any big thing would do ; but they would touch nothing. It was literally heart-breaking. It was like some nightmare in which one is always just going to get free and never does. I tried everything—orange quills, Wickhams, variants, sedges ; they would sail in a straight line up to my fly, taking the natural one on this side of it, make a loop round mine, and start feeding again on the other side. Not one but forty fish did this. I can even now recall the trembling of my knees and the choking sounds in my throat, as I cursed them and the lake and the moon —the last especially, for it was probably she who did it. She was up during the whole rise and I never knew a trout that could look her in the face and run after strange gods at the same time. Whatever the cause, they had some occult power of selection which seemed never to fail them even in that wild hour of surfeit. The way they walked along their path and stepped aside to let the drunkard pass and picked up the trail again was quasi-human. It was the late evening counterpart of the early morning rise in the mist on the Test, of which I spoke before, and gave me an even more unhuman sense of having stolen by stealth into some mysterious orgy of the underworld, to stand there a mere spectator, ridiculous, despised and ashamed. The dark lake with the deep purple glow upon it, the sudden upheaval of the waters, the sucking and hurrying and deliberation, the picking of the sheep from the goats, the great white moon and the feeling of silence. Perhaps they do this every night when the word goes round that the enemy is asleep, and just this once the fairies forgot us and found us there when it was too late and the revel had begun. Or were they laughing at the three wise mortals who had said they were no more, and staged this little comedy for the earth folk ?

I had one amusing experience with the dry-fly there in 1922. I was supposed to be fishing the deep lagoon at the Butcombe end, but it was very hot and sunny and I was really lying on the bank basking and smoking. Presently I became aware of a slight wave lapping the shore of the pool on my left. I cast a dry " Victor " on to the spot which I calculated was the middle of the ring, and awaited events like a punt-fisher with a float. Nothing happened for some time, and then far down in the depths I saw a spot of white. It grew gradually larger and more luminous—it reminded me of the approaching motor-headlights at night on the " movies "—and finally divided into two and proceeded to swallow my fly. This was surprising enough, but the fish, when he found he was hooked, darted into a cave under my bank, and wedged himself tight. Hand-lining and prodding him with the landing-net had no effect. As luck would have it, I saw two young men on a bridge close by and I called them to my help. One held the rod and the other held me (stripped nearly to the waist), and I retrieved him with my hand from the bowels of the earth.

Like all loughs Blagdon is at the mercy of the weather, and in a calm or when the clouds are low you might as well throw your hat into the water at most times of the day. I calculated during one of these lean periods—by counting the number of times I threw a fly in ten minutes, and the number of hours I stuck to it—that I had had 20,000 casts for one fish! On the other hand you never know your luck—you may at any moment meet with some yawning "stickle-backer" who has roused himself from sleep below and started out in search of adventure.

This phase of Blagdon luck once seriously annoyed me. Sheringham and that same nephew of mine and I had been there a whole week, and had all three drawn blank so far as the lake was concerned. Sheringham had served some small purpose in the scheme of things. He spent a lot of his time with a six-foot rod groping through jungles of brambles in a little stream below the dam, catapulting flies into likely places over trout that had never seen a human being since they were spawned. He would turn up at the farm at various times of the day, bruised and dirty and bleeding, but invariably with something for the pot, so that we regarded him with amused tolerance as a minor bene-factor until the last day; then our feelings underwent a change. We had all three agreed to give it up and go home, but at the last moment Sheringham said he would stay on over the week-end. My nephew and I sat on a bench by the dam, while we waited for the train, and jeered at him as he flogged the dead horse. Just as we got up to go, throwing a few extra-sarcastic commiserations over our shoulders, he hooked (and subsequently landed) a 4½-pounder. It was particu-larly rough on me, for not only were my clothes packed and in the train already, but I was being par-ticularly funny, as I thought, at the time. Sheringham was perfectly happy sitting in a punt watching a float for hours at a time on the chance of flicking a two-inch pinkeen over his shoulder (I would rather have my teeth slowly extracted one by one; but he was not so accustomed to concentrated excitement as I am), and I had just made some humorous suggestions about kegs of beer and sleep and the other amenities of coarse fishing when this happened. My nephew has not forgotten it, as I know to my cost.

I love Blagdon, not only because it holds great fish, but because I have always been happy there. It would be impossible to find more delightful people than those of the farm who have always taken me in as their guest. I have a vivid recollection, too, of the time, in the middle of the war when we were most severely rationed, when I arrived there starved and tired to death after weeks of work and drill, and sat down to potato-soup, a wild duck, a black-currant pudding, a local " Wensleydale " cheese and as much cider as I wanted—all farm-grown. But they were (and are) part and parcel of that lovely spot in Somerset typical of southern England at its best.

Blagdon is an artificial reservoir, it is true, but it is only the western end that lets you into that secret. Here is the big embankment of which Sheringham speaks in *Trout-fishing*, where the " great whales " lie with their noses on the stones. But you can sit on the grass in a dozen places round the shore and swear that you are on the banks of one of the prettiest natural lakes in the kingdom. There is not a lovelier sight (*pace* Ramsbury and Hurstbourne Priors in buttercup-time) in England than Blagdon from the Butcombe end at sundown, with the tiny town straggling up the steep hill-side like a Bavarian village, the red roofs of the houses peeping out of the thick orchards (with never a Methodist Chapel to shock the artist's eye), and the evening sunlight setting the windows of the old church aglow and flushing with purple-pink the glassy surface of the lake. There is a stillness here that belongs to no other valley. You can hear the " plop " of the big trout far out half a mile away. You can talk to your friend across the water when the sun is down without ever raising your voice, and hear the scream of his reel in the blackness, and Blagdon is about seven miles round, and he may be half the length of the lake from you.

But the dominant impression in my mind is the lovely colour of the evening light upon the valley as you face it looking east. It has a crimson velvet glow which hangs like an aura on the meadows and makes the shores and the scolloped hills burn with fires. It is Devonshire clay here, and the whole landscape warms pink and deepens to purple-black as the sun sinks low.

I know, too, that there was once a witch in the valley and that they drowned her when they let the water in ; and one night as I grope my way home in the dark I shall stumble on Hänsel and Gretel asleep on the grass in a mist of white angels, with the myriad million stars of the Milky Way and the golden lights of Blagdon shining on their heads and winking in the watery glass at their feet.

XV

BLAGDON (*continued*)

YOU can fish at Blagdon as late as you like, but I never feel that this "dark" fishing is fair sport or that the "fuzzy-buzzy" type of lure is really fishing at all. Still there is unquestionably a devilish excitement beating in the heart of black night, whether you are fishing or poaching or playing hide-and-seek. The silent pull in the darkness by the embankment at Blagdon is as potent a destroyer of conscience as a pull of wood-alcohol.

There are very few of us who have not poached at one time or other of our lives—especially if we happen to have been born in Ireland—from tickling a trout onward. I was initiated into various mysteries of the art when I was a schoolboy home for the holidays in Kilkenny. There was a boy in Thomastown village who was the greatest master of the craft I ever came across. He taught me numbers of crimes, from damming up streams and leaving the trout high and dry to pulling a rabbit out of a hole with a briar. One eschews such barbarisms as one grows up, but there is a devilish lawlessness about them which fascinates the small boy trained on Fenimore Cooper and *The Old Shikarri*.

The biter was sometimes bit, however. I used to spear the eels under the stones in the Nore with a fork, and was much grieved because they took so long to die, and I asked my instructor how I could get them to accelerate their end. He told me (it was the only mistake he made, if it was a mistake !) that the best way to kill them was to bite their tails. I tried it once (what it is to be young !) and no more, for it promptly turned round and bit me on the lip.

I had an experience of a different sort with eels one spring on another Irish river, the Blackwater in Co. Waterford. I had given the salmon up in despair and had gone back to the trout. I was standing up to my waist in the middle of the river and my ghillie was fast asleep on the bank. I had been having wonderful sport. They were taking splendidly and I felt that the Blackwater was as inexhaustible as the Leprechaun's shilling, when all of a sudden the whole thing stopped. There was nothing that I could see to account for it, and I was bewildered. I went on flogging the river, but nothing happened. Presently the ghillie woke up and began to fill his pipe. I saw him suddenly freeze to attention and stare into the water at his feet. " Ye may come in, sir," he said. " Ye'll get no more fish to-day. The luogs is comin' up."

It was quite true. As I got to the shore I saw the little elvers coming up in millions. They were swimming up in lines of quasi-military formation, hugging the banks and pressing on to some destination, driven by their instincts and oblivious to danger. And danger there was, for from that moment when they first appeared till the last platoon had gone by, there was not a fish in the river that had not filled himself to repletion with them.

Whenever I think of Blagdon I murmur curses on the so-called education of my young days. Why was I never taught the elements of painting ? If I had had some sort of grounding in that branch of art I should not have to grind my teeth for impotence to put on canvas the beauty that I see with my eyes and can never express. In those days music and painting were for the few. They were looked on as esoteric gifts, harmful as often as not, to be encouraged, maybe, as an amateur accomplishment. It had never occurred to mankind in general that these gifts were not particular, but that all children might have them hidden in their minds waiting for encouragement to emerge.

We know now that every normal child has music in him and a voice to sing with, and that, no matter how irresponsive he may be at first, and however shy those gifts may be, they can be reached and coaxed out of him through the appeal of imagination. Mr. Walter Ford told me of his experience with a choir of Liverpool slum-children. He had gone down (officially, I think; some far-sighted pioneer in the Education Office had sent him) to see at first-hand some experiments which were being made there on these lines. He described to me vividly the scene when those children, who had been yelling at one another in awful nasal strident voices, were first asked to sing a tune. There was a moment of stunned silence and then a roar of laughter. They literally did not know one note from another. Half of them could not even say whether the top C was higher than the bottom one. He said he would never forget the clatter of ridicule which drowned the first attempt. And yet, when he returned in about three months' time, the very same children were singing folk-songs in unison with a beauty of tone and a purity of language that actually made him cry, hardened old singer as he was himself.

It is true that the particular trainer in this case was a genius. He and his daughters had the strange magnetism and the priceless gift of imagination themselves and the power to reach it in the children, and it was by that appeal alone they had won them. But that is beside the point. The main thing is that music is born in us all, and is only waiting encouragement to come out. Never mind how unpromising the material may look—there may be a star in any dust-heap.

I know of another instance in my own experience. One of our neighbours in the country heard me tell the Liverpool story. She had a small son, aged six, who had never shown any interest in music, although his mother played the piano very well. She had naturally supposed that it was left out of his composition and had made no attempt to cultivate it. She asked us whether, just for experiment, we would let our governess go over once or twice and try her hand on the raw material. Of course, we agreed and off the governess went, full of excitement at the idea. Up to that time the boy had amused himself in the usual way small boys do, by putting the coal in the piano, or holding the cat up by the tail or pulling the tea-things into his lap. He received her with polite frigidity. At the end of a fortnight he was waiting for her on the steps in a state of throbbing excitement an hour before she arrived !

That country child and those Liverpool children— far as the poles apart in their environment—would never have known that blessed possession was theirs if someone had not found it for them ; and who knows but that I, *ceteris paribus*, might not have had the same power to capture and keep the glory of the Blagdon sunset and the fairy lights of its twin firmament.

Night-fishing makes one ready for supper and that means much tobacco and much talk, and one sleeps as though drugged by an opiate. I can only once remember failing to go to sleep within five minutes at Blagdon. I had just got into bed and blown out the light and was drowsily settling down when I became aware of a phosphorescent light moving slowly up the pillow beside me. I thought at first that I was already asleep and that someone was drawing a luminous " fuzzy-buzzy " in front of my nose, but found that I was disgustingly wide awake and distinctly disturbed by the apparition, which was pursuing its course unconcernedly. I thought for a moment that it was some vagary of moonlight through the blind, but then remembered there was no moon, so I promptly hit out and it promptly vanished. I lit my candle and searched, but could find nothing and I went to sleep. Next morning I found under the bolster a small centipede-like creature curled up like an adder. It was, I gather, a familiar centipede, which leaves the phosphorescent trail I saw, and which is quite harmless. I was almost as much annoyed by it as a friend of mine was by the Winchester police who refused to recognise glow-worms as an adequate substitute for paraffin in his bicycle-lamp.

Sleep once played me false there in the day-time. When the fish are sulking and you are tired of doing nothing you can lie down anywhere on the slopes at Blagdon and doze comfortably off. I am very lucky in that I can go to sleep at any time in a straight-backed chair in two minutes. On this particular occasion I had been sitting on the stone embankment where it curls round from the dam, watching for a big fish I knew of to come in after the sticklebacks in the weeds below me. The slope I was on was a hard granite wall, but it might have been a feather bed, as sleep overcame me and I gently sank back and off into dreams. And then in a moment I awoke. My sixth sense had rung the alarm-bell. The big fellow was chasing the sticklebacks about forty yards away. I was wide awake, as I thought, and I stalked round him and got into the water twenty yards, as I thought, behind him, and I literally walked on top of him. I was terrified, far more so than he, and I believe I yelled, and I am not ashamed of it.

Some few years ago, in the *Salmon and Trout Magazine*, Captain Dunne gave an illuminating and fascinating account of the habits and customs of the shore-hugging sticklebacker at Blagdon, telling us how each great fish had his regular rounds, returning to each weed-patch at an average interval of about twenty-five minutes, and how each time the sticklebacks gave you warning of his approach by the commotion they made in the water. But not even he, nor any other writer, could put on paper the tense excitement which the man with the rod feels as he waits for his arrival. Walking up to the spot in the roots where the covey has settled or waiting at the point of the wood for the first burst of the pheasants is electric enough, but neither is a patch on the anticipation of the advent of the sticklebacker. For when at last you see him make his first raid it is as likely as not that you will get him. You need not be too particular—at least, that is my experience—or take too long about your cast ; remember he is a traveller and will not wait for you. You have only got to throw the fly within reasonable distance of him, and if he is looking that way, he will do the rest. Exactly—*he will do the rest*. You will see a miniature racing motor-boat rush through the water at your fly, throwing a great wave up on either side, and if you leave it to him he is yours. I know of no set of circumstances in which reason and impulse are at such deadly enmity. Every fibre of your body calls out " Strike ! " the moment he reaches it, while cold common-sense says, " Give him time ! " It is not a question either of

L

ordinary time but oceans of time ! If you strike at the moment when he seems to seize your fly you will not even touch him once in a hundred times. He evidently keeps his mouth open for a considerable while after taking it, and you have got to wait till he closes it. It requires an almost superhuman power of control, for that first long rush is liable to shake down the best of resolutions like a house of cards ; but when you do strike strike with a vengeance. I once measured such an individual rush and found it to be roughly twelve feet, which goes to prove the theory that fish, even if they cannot actually see the object at long range, are at any rate aware of its presence.

This peripatetic habit of the Blagdon trout is the only thing in the place that makes for monotony. You can, if you will, walk up and down the shore merely for the sake of variety, but for fish-catching purposes you will do better to get out to one of the points where the bank juts out into the water, and stay there and cast regularly. It is the fish who travels, not you, and you are fairly sure to intercept him on his beat at one of these points, since he is not going to go farther out of his way than is necessary to get from one weed-bed to another. His mentality, or at least his habit of action, is very interesting. He will play a lone hand, apparently, for one half of the day, and then will go off on a hunting expedition with his fellows for the other. You may see him on his visiting rounds in the morning and never get a glimpse of him in the afternoon ; and you may hear at tea-time in the hut that he has been seen in company with other bandits working a particular bank where no one happened to be fishing. You go to the bank in question in the evening only to find that trout have apparently deserted the lake. You may go to the Butcombe lagoon one sundown and find them there in shoals and even have a chance with a dry-fly, and two evenings afterwards the same water may be like the pool in Miss Coleridge's *Witches' Wood*:

"As though a scare had frightened off the eye of day."

It is always a toss-up at Blagdon, and that is the fun of it. If it were a regular thing, the Bristol Saturday "midnighters" would have reduced it to a certainty long ago and the sporadic visitor would be left out in the cold; but as a matter of fact he is almost as likely to run up against a good thing as the people who know the proved places.

The actual technique of the work is, of course, as in all lake-fishing, monotonous. In the day-time you let your fly sink after casting, and draw it in gradually towards you by raising the point of the rod and gathering in the slack with your left hand; at night you pull the fly along the surface of the water from the start.* This is the only real variety in it, since, of course, whatever movement the fly makes must be given to it by the fisherman. The Blagdon trout is a gentle striker, especially at night. You have to do it for him and strike quickly and hard at the least sign of a pull. The night fish feels something like the Spey salmon— as though you had hung up in a snag—and it is not till you have struck him yourself that you feel his weight. Every now and again you meet with the other sort, but even the sticklebacker pulls up suddenly at the end of his dizzy rush and takes the fly gingerly.

There is none of the fine work of the 4X cast and the old-timer and the perils of the weed-bed, and there is no running water to dance your fly along, but there is the blessed thought that you never can tell your

---

* This night technique is not invariable. It changes from season to season.

luck, the perfectly justifiable hope that at any moment, anywhere, under any adverse conditions, you may run up against the fish of your life. He may be just strolling along on his round of visits, he may be out on the " Bummel," and too hilarious to be discreet, he may be simply an investigator keen on research, he may be hunting with the pack, or, fiercest, biggest, wariest of them all, he may have sneaked out just at sundown from behind the sunken tree-stump in the watercourse, where he has lain all day in the dark. Whoever he is, and whenever he turns up, he will be as good a man as you and generally better.

A fresh water supply was turned into the lake some time ago; this will, I understand, have the effect of keeping it permanently at the same level. It is impossible to tell yet what effect it will have upon the fishing, but by the ordinary rules it should be all to the good. It may rejuvenate some of the old monsters who have, no doubt, for some time past led a catfish-like existence on the bottom of the lake and bring them forth to explore again the haunts of their youth. It may even reawaken the famous evening rise. We cannot say ; it is on the knees of the gods. But Blagdon itself will always remain one of the few places where the hand of man has improved on nature, bewitching in its beauty, with its Bavarian village, its purple sunsets, its nights with the thousand eyes, its kindly people, its virile sport and its blessed physical fatigue.

XVI

THE FISHERMAN'S CURSES

ISHING is a real test of character. Your spirits are either on top of a mountain or in the depths of a pit, with certain dead-levels of boredom and commonplace, supposing your soul craves for poundage alone. But there are many sufferings and humiliations outside the orthodox annoyances of the atrocious British climate : the fly in the small of your back which you have to undress yourself to get at ; the broken Thermos bottle ; the disintegrated lunch, bulls, wasps' nests, moor-hens at the wrong moment, cockchafers in your eye, the other man round the corner at the very spot you have been working up to all the morning, the cast which doubles back, the matches which you have left at home and, worst of all, water in your waders.

Of all the maddening things the worst is falling into the water. I have fallen into the Spey three times—near the bank each time, fortunately, for the Spey is in such a hurry to get you to the sea that it does not give you any time to stop and think. In fact, I made such a habit of it that I gave up wearing my watch and left it at home. I was not much the worse for it except for badly damaging one of my fingers in an attempt to link up with Mother Earth, but to have your tobacco and cigarettes made into a wet mush and to feel the icy water trickle gradually from your waist to your toes is enough to bolshevise a saint, especially as it means either walking home a couple of miles to change your things or inviting double pneumonia.

The wonder is that you can wade in the Spey at all. It runs like a mill-race, and the bottom is covered with rocks varying in size from a parched pea to a Roman encampment and in shape from a marble to a cubist portrait. At low water these are covered with slime, and a limpet or an anemone would slide about on them as on roller-skates. In view of the precariousness of the foothold and the enthusiasm of the water, the Spey wader should be equipped with a Gieve waistcoat, an air-balloon, and a wire hawser attached to a ghillie or a derrick, on shore, and should have a portable hot-coffee machine keeping pace with him on the bank with a spare set of clothes in the oven. As it is, he has to put up with a pole with which to prod the immediate future, and which at one moment runs up against the rock of Gibraltar and the next descends into the bowels of Vesuvius.

Salmon-waders are bad enough; still, if you have been trained as an acrobat you can sometimes get up before the water has had time to get through your belt and you can always hurl your coat out on to the bank to dry; but short waders are simply man-traps. To begin with, they sag a good two inches unbeknownst to you after the first ten minutes in the water. They start as high as your own spirits when you both set out for the day, but fall victims to acute depression in a very short time, so that the pool you stood up in in the early part of the morning with a comfortable margin laps gently over your knees and down to your feet later on in the day. There are two other ways of getting your waders full even in shallow water: one by stepping backwards and hitting your heel against a stone; the other by trying to crawl out up the bank with both hands full. It is no doubt auto-suggestion, but the mere fact of having no hand to save you coats the bank with lubricating oil, opens fissures in the bed of the stream, strips the top of everything except nettles, and fills the river with a cloudburst. The pain of trying to hold on with one's elbows as they rake the flints while your feet slide out in a curve in midstream is only surpassed by the ignominy. There is no more pitiable sight than a grown man sitting on a wasps' nest pouring the water out of his waders. I speak from experience.

I never know why one deliberately looks for trouble by fishing at all, or invites these abominable discomforts by getting into cold water when there is no necessity for it. The ideal existence is, of course, that of the giant tortoise at the Zoo. He sleeps placidly through the pestilential English winter in a nice hot room, and when he wakes up finds his meals all ready for him without having to pay for them. He has not got to shave in the morning, or wash his teeth, or attend rehearsals, or take his clothes off at night or, worse still, put them on again next day, or find yellow envelopes marked " Income Tax—Private " by his bed every morning when he opens his eyes. There is, unfortunately, no prospect of any benevolent society taking such a generous view of my scientific value, but if a friendly Turkish bath would undertake to give me a comfortable home for the rest of my days, I would promise never again to inflict myself upon the public, and I should never again have to shiver in green-rooms waiting for my turn to go on. (I once told Hans Richter that I hated the Leonora Overture worse than any other piece of music in the world. He became apoplectic and only quieted down when I explained that I was referring to the number of times

I had had to listen to it in the distance, while I waited my turn to come on.) But I have a sneaking idea that even as I lay tucked up in hot towels the remembrance would come back to me of a certain day when I started to motor down with Merric Bovill for a week at Stockbridge.

As we crawled through the traffic at Hammersmith I adored the trams—the most abominable of all forms of locomotion; I showered blessings on the very buses I had objurgated before with clenched fists; I chaffed the small boys who tried to get run over; I inhaled the dust of the motor-lorry in front as though it had been the elixir of life; and when our tyres burst I laughed for sheer *joie de vivre* and rolled up my sleeves and spat on my hands and worked the jack. I was like a schoolboy the night before his first holidays, setting up my rod before going to bed so as not to lose a minute in the morning, and when I went to sleep the tortoise was nowhere.

That was a wonderful week. It was early August, and we had the whole river to ourselves. We fished a different beat every day, the weather was gorgeous and there was a rise, off and on, the whole time, and the days passed like a dream. But we nearly paid for it in the end, for my host fell asleep on the way back as we were crossing a bridge near Woking, and if I had not shouted and grabbed the steering-wheel we should have ended our days in the canal with our heads in the mud and our heels in the air.

Stockbridge certainly is a wonderful place; miles of water, beautifully kept, each beat different in character, and every beat holding great fish, and not an easy one among them; a rise of some sort at some time of the day, or all day, and an unfailing evening rise when the blue-winged olives appear and the orange-quills bring up the big ones ; and the infinite variety of the various stretches. I think I like the Park stream best of all the beats, for it seems remote from the world and though you do not see so many fish as, say, in the Grosvenor water, there is an absence of fuss, a leisurely atmosphere about it, which leaves you in peace to devote yourself to your fish till you either get him or put him down. There is something fascinating, too, about the light. Your head-and-tailer rolls over in such a lazy way that you can see every spot on his body, and you feel he must soon be in your basket. You can cover most of the water, too, without much trouble.

I remember one fish there with disgust. He lay on the far side in an indentation in the bank and was rising at everything that came along. I reached him every time I cast and invariably brought him up, but though I tried every dodge I knew, the stream bellied the line and pulled the fly out of his mouth at the critical moment. He was the most confiding fish for a Stockbridge trout I ever saw. I determined at last to cross the river and fish him from below on his own side, so I walked down a few hundred yards to a bridge, and came up to him on the far bank.

He was a beauty of about 3 lbs. and in grand condi-tion. He rose at once and I missed him and caught my fly in the grass behind me, and as I was gently tugging at it, I became aware of a subdued murmur all round me and found I was kneeling in the middle of a wasps' nest. We both went " down " at the same moment.

I had two amusing (now, not then) experiences with the true fisherman's curse, namely bulls. One was on the Test at the bottom of the Hurstbourne water. I was calmly fishing below one of the cow-bridges, at peace with all the world except the two-pounder I was after, when a bull suddenly appeared on top of the bank immediately opposite. After taking one ferocious look at me he slid down the side and made for me at a hand gallop. I made one frenzied bolt and leaped over a fence, dragging my rod and line after me, anyhow, only to see the bull stroll gently up to the river, take a long drink and stroll quietly back again the way he came. It is very funny now, but it made me very angry at the time, though I cannot quite explain why.

The other occasion was on the upper Ramsbury Manor water on the Kennet. I had just got over a fence in the middle of a thick hedge and found myself confronted by three bulls. They plunged at once into the water and swam across to the far bank and were as promptly chivvied back again by a cowman on the other side. This battledore and shuttlecock lasted for the better part of an afternoon. Fortunately for me the attention of the three Leanders was so focused on the distant Hero in the far meadow that they did not bother about me, but the Hellespont became rather too turgid for a dry-fly purist.

Thunderstorms have a bad reputation as spoilers of sport, but that is not my experience. They can be very uncomfortable and feel very dangerous, it is true. I once walked home two miles in the Black Forest when the whole air was a throbbing sheet of flame, and the lightning played round my rod, and I was never more frightened in my life. But I have had wonderful sport in the very thick of a thunderstorm. It keeps fish down, no doubt, at first, when the clouds are low, especially in loughs, but once it breaks the tension seems to break with it and when the rain comes down the fish come up. I had a furious half-hour once in the Ardennes. I had not had a pull all day (I was fishing wet), when suddenly a thunderstorm broke over us, and the river literally went mad on the spot. I got eleven fish of over a pound in half an hour, and then got into a big one ($2\frac{1}{2}$ lbs.), and at the same moment my reel jammed and for ten minutes I raced up and down the bank, plunging in and out of the water, to the bewilderment of my brother, who thought I had hooked an otter.

This particular fishing was great fun. It was some distance from Diekirch, where we were staying, and we used to start about six in the morning and get breakfast at a junction where we had the best part of an hour to wait for a train. We had the most delicious coffee at that little station that we ever tasted, and we used to talk of it to the others in awed whispers. One day, as I was looking out of the window of the waiting-room, I saw our hostess hurry along the platform with the coffee-pot in her hand, and turn one of the taps of the engine into it. *Omne ignotum pro magnifico.*

Of course, one's reel should never jam. I anticipate the homilies which the bare idea invokes. But one's reel sometimes *does* jam, and that's all there is about it. You may oil it and re-wind it and wrap it up for the winter in cotton wool in a warm room, and the first two-pounder you hook in the spring, the check snaps, the ball-bearings disintegrate, the line forms the figure of 8, and heads south instead of north, and as on such occasions you have forgotten to bring a spare one with you, your day is done for.

But there is another curse with which it is afflicted— the foot of man. Sheringham speaks in *Trout-fishing* of a certain southern river (the rack would not make me disclose its identity) which is given up to such common truck as chub and the like, but which shelters a small colony of ancient aristocrats which emerge once a year from their castle and show themselves to the public.

This, being interpreted, means that in one particular spot in this river there are a few great trout which show up in Mayfly time. They are reputed, or were reputed, to run up to 10 lbs. That was some years ago, and they are probably a good deal bigger now. I cannot say myself, for I never saw them; I only felt them.

Sheringham and I had sneaked off there one week-end in early June. Secrecy was essential. He had gone to study the habits of the Lapland salmon and I was fulfilling a concert engagement in the Hebrides. He insisted that he was more or less of the host for the first day and sent me off to the famous spot, while he diggled for sticklebacks or some of the other coarse fish his heart yearned after. It was about two miles down the river and I was very hot and very excited, for the Mayfly was thick on the water and now, if ever, the giants might appear. I laid my rod on the ground (I anticipate questions as to what a spike is useful for) far from the edge of the bank, sat down on a stump, lit my pipe, and at the same moment saw a mighty wave from a submerged shoulder move up the river like a Severn bore. I leaped to my feet, crash went the bough I was sitting on, and down went my heel with 14½ stone on top of it on to my reel.

It was a horrible sight. The outer plate looked like a birch-bark canoe, the handle stood out at an angle of forty-five like a bookie's top-hat, and the balls of the bearings were chasing one another like the quick-silver in a Christmas-tree puzzle. I am quite aware that all I had to do was to open my bag and get out the spanner and the tweezers and the acetylene crib-cracking plant, and the cobbler's wax and screws which I always carry on fishing expeditions, or failing these, my spare reel. But I did not have a spare reel or anything else in my bag except an inadequate lunch. My whole repair outfit was a small stone which some kind earthquake had deposited in the middle of a quaking water-meadow.

I hammered and tinkered with this for nearly three hours. I have a dim recollection of wanting to whimper like a dog, for there appeared to be a school of porpoises at play in the river the whole time I was at work, and I was powerless to join in the fun. I finished the job at last, and I am bound to say it was a masterpiece. The reel sang like a cricket, but the moment they heard it they went down. But there was worse to come. I got into three of them in the evening and lost them all. It was the same process in each case. They took my fly, ran up about fifteen yards and then calmly spat it out. I had been fishing with duns all the season and had forgotten all about their horny jaws and Mayfly casts and had handled them with a 4X touch !

Talking of otters, I had a strange experience at Stockbridge in 1921. I was fishing the meadows at the very top of the water in the late evening. The river here takes two almost right-angle turns, and at the first of these there is a hatch. As I came up to it I heard two separate " soups " from big feeding fish, and could just make out in the dark two rises at the top and bottom of the back eddy respectively. I went round and tried for the upper one first and got him (he was 3 lbs.), and started at once on the one lower down. As I was actually taking the fly back for the cast there was a terrific splash and churning up of the water in the exact spot where he was rising, and that was the end of him. It certainly was not a pike and almost as certainly was an otter, for the keeper had seen one about there a little while before. The otter is a silent hunter as a rule, but it is possible that at night he was more careless, or perhaps he knew that he must hurry up if he wanted to get there first.

I have several times accidentally hooked birds in the air (not to speak of ghillies), but with one exception I have never done them any serious damage. The exception was a tragic one and almost as uncanny in its circumstances as that evening rise at Blagdon. I was having lunch at my favourite place by the scolloped bank at the bottom of the fishing on the Test, and had stuck my rod into the ground a few yards away. I noticed presently that my fly had come loose and was blowing about in the wind. The swifts were sweeping about in great numbers and it flashed through my mind that one of them might possibly foul it. It never occurred to me that one of them would actually take it. I had never known them make a mistake. The chances of any mishap were so remote that I left the fly blowing loose rather than take the trouble of getting up from my comfortable corner, but I remember saying to myself that if one of them did run up against it I should hear the reel go, and at the actual moment the idea was passing through my mind the reel went. There was a swift on the end of the line. Poor little beast ! It was caught in the tongue and I had to kill it. I have never forgiven myself for it ; it was sheer laziness on my part which had made it possible. This is the only occasion in my life when I have seen a bird make a mistake. I have known the swallows so thick on the water in a heavy rise of fly that I have been almost afraid to cast for fear of foul-hooking one of them, but I have never seen one of them touch the artificial fly, though it must have looked the fattest and most tempting of the lot.

I have heard people recount with glee how they have hooked and landed a water-rat. To begin with, the hooking of a water-rat requires no more skill than hailing a bus, and what satisfaction they can get in hauling that terrified whistling little friend ashore passes my comprehension. He has given us all disappointments without number. How often have we crawled up to that ring under the bank which we have been waiting for for so long, only to see him come out with a twinkle in his eye and swim across to the far side ! But however hard we may objurgate him, he will always be one of the most lovable of all our river-companions.

Sharkey once had an encounter with a water-rat which was very similar to my experience with the swift. He was fishing " blind " in a hatch-hole for a particular fish which lived there and was delighted when, as he thought, he hooked him. He was rather puzzled at the very unorthodox way in which he behaved, until he found that it was a water-rat hooked in the tongue. Sharkey was just as fond of them as I, and he meant him to have his life if a doctor could save him. He told me that he had an anxious time with him ; he fought like a dog and the difficulty was to prevent him from impaling himself on the scissors. He had to make jabs at him whenever he could, and by good luck (and skill no doubt) one snip went right and the fly came away and the little chap went off not much the worse.

XVII

DOGS AND HORSES

IN one thing we were unlucky at Hurstbourne—
we had four tragedies with our dogs. Two were
run over by motor cars, one was poisoned and one was
killed by another dog. All four were Scotch terriers.
The circumstances of the first two murders are almost
unbelievable in England. Both dogs were run over
when out with the nurse and children, and in each case
the people drove on and left them to die on the road in
front of their owners' eyes. There was no doubt about
their being aware of what they had done, for in one
instance they stood up in the car and looked back, and
in the other they actually stopped for a moment or two
as if to help and then thought better of it and drove
on.

I did my best to run them to earth and *The Times*
and *The Car* most kindly helped me, but the only
response I got was the inevitable letter from Mr.
Bernard Shaw to the latter paper to say that the right
thing to do when you ran over a dog was to run away.
It is inconceivable that anyone who has had children
of his own or lived with dogs could leave a small
terrier to die in convulsions before the eyes of the
children who loved it. I trust that their tyres have burst
and their dogs have bitten them from that day to this!

We had also a big Aberdeen, but he was an extraordinary dog, and became so dangerous that we had to
send him to live at Highnam, my father-in-law's house

near Gloucester. There were about three people in the world he was friends with and we could do what we liked with him, but he bit everybody else indiscriminately. One would have supposed that he would have been surreptitiously made away with by somebody or other, but he had some occult power of inspiring respect and affection even in the people who were most afraid of him, and he died of old age.

He was better than any spaniel I ever knew in searching a covert, and if he came out at the far end looking unconcerned you could be certain there was not a rabbit in the place. I never knew him make a mistake about this and trusted his word implicitly. Fighting was his joy, and every few weeks he would go for a scrap with a half-bull terrier at an inn on the way to Gloucester. The routine was always the same. He would disappear in the evening and be found outside the house next morning with one eye closed and one ear hanging in shreds and various gashes about his body, but bursting with pride and good temper. When I see the miserable crowd of Poms and Griffons and Pekingese and other effeminate lap-dogs I think of Joe and the Dog Inn on the Gloucester road and thank God for a man. He lived in the stable as a rule, but when we were at Highnam he spent the day with us in the house, on the presumption that he would go back to the stable at night. Every evening when his bed-time came he was nowhere to be found. They searched the house high and low, but there was never a sign of him, though they called and whistled for him everywhere; but just before I blew out my candle Joe would walk out from under my bed and he and I would sit in front of the fire and laugh till we ached.

I met later a dog which reminded me of Joe. He was a Sealyham belonging to Colonel Llewellyn, spoken

M

of earlier. His appearance was deceptive. He was sweetness personified to look at and butter would not melt in his mouth, but he would rather bite you than not. I was no exception to the rule, but in my case it was a mistake for which he expressed deep contrition.

Llewellyn and I in that summer (August 1923) had intended to join Harford and try some fishing which we had heard of in the North of England. He was to call for me with his car, and we were to motor the whole way. About an hour before he was due I received a letter which made the northern trip impossible, and I broke it to Llewellyn as soon as he arrived.

" All right," he said. " Jump in. We'll go back to Wiltshire." And in I jumped on top of " Gillie," who was lying on the floor of the car. Gillie's horizon on motoring trips up to that time had been bounded by brakes and gears and self-starters, and his dog-senses had been wasted on petrol and oil and boot-blacking. It had never occurred to him that you could see out of a motor at all.

In two seconds I had him on my knee and from that moment we were sworn friends. A new life opened to him. That and every subsequent journey was a frenzied orgy of growls and yells and attempted plunges through the window at other dogs, with paint-scratching thrown in. His eyes, when he asked to be taken on to one's knee, were deep yellow wells of pathetic gentleness ; but he fought every dog he saw, from the Italian-greyhound-cum-fox-terrier who put his beaming nose inside the front door 'of the inn at Upavon and said, " Hullo ! how's everybody ? " to the sheep dog who was his unwilling, but courteous, host at the farm at Blagdon.

He would lie on the bank at the latter place and guard our belongings for hours at a stretch, and when

one of us hooked a fish he would swim out in the
pitch dark to help us to land it. He was not so welcome
then as at a later hour. Blagdon can be as dark as
Erebus, and if you have not got a torch with you you
may grope about for an indefinite period. But Gillie,
when supper-time came, would run a couple of yards
ahead of us and take us home by the shortest route. He
never made a mistake ; we just " followed the gleam."

There is, of course, one dog in any one man's life,
and mine belonged to my boyhood. He was a Kerry
blue, in so far as you could credit him with any definite
breed, but he made up for his pedigree with his dis-
position. I bought him from a well-known dog-
stealer in Dublin. He was unquestionably the ugliest
dog in the bunch, but it was a case of mutual love at
first sight. He promised me with his eyes the moment
I saw him that if I would take him away with me he
would be my friend for life, and so he was. He was
and he wasn't, though the single " wasn't " wasn't his
fault. He was the worst complication in the serious
illness I spoke of earlier, for a week before I reached
home he had got himself stolen again. They told me
afterwards that once they had pulled me round the
corner they could get me no farther and that I lay there
for weeks inert, without any apparent interest in life ;
and then the maternal instinct found the solution.
They sent out and searched the slums of Dublin with
a fine comb, and one day the door of my room burst
open and he rushed in and leapt on my bed and from
that moment I never looked back.

He travelled all through Germany with me, and
spent a winter and spring in Florence. At the latter
place we lived in a flat at the top of a high building. He
used to take a flying leap out of the room on to the
window-sill outside, put on the brakes suddenly, and

then quietly stretch himself full length in the sun on a ledge about a foot wide and eighty feet from the ground. He slept every night of his life on the end of my bed, and swore at me in a terrifying way every time I moved my feet. He shut the door and rang the bell, with worryings and growls, and pretended that each order you gave him would be your last. There was nothing he loved so much as having a cracker—not the Christmas-tree variety, but the explosive repeater squib—tied on to his tail. The ordinary dog under similar circumstances would be off to the next county in five seconds and never come back ; but at the very mention of fireworks he would come tearing up and ask for it, swearing at us and biting us for not hurrying up, and would then chase his tail round and round snapping at the bursts and barking in delirious excitement.

He was not a dog who paraded his pluck ; he just seemed to be indifferent to danger—*vide* his Florentine exploits. The only time I ever saw him really frightened was when he fell off a five-foot wall into a pigsty where there was an old sow and a dozen boneens. His return over that wall was the finest bit of speeding-up he ever did.

This quality of superior aloofness made him the envy of each and every one of my myriad cousins who possessed a dog of regulation pattern, and the rubbing-in of his virtues has hardly been forgiven to this day. One of these cousins asked me to write something in her birthday-book. She naturally supposed I would laboriously transcribe some aria out of *The Magic Flute*, and her impotent fury when she found a masterly poem tabulating the virtues of Punch and the degrading vices of Tycho was one of the successes of my life.

He would lie in front of the fire until he was red-hot
and then fling himself panting against the crack of the
door, so as to get the draught along his spine, and
when he was thoroughly chilled would come back to
the fire, and ring the Turkish bath changes *ad infinitum*.
I know that this was all wrong and that he should
have lain in his appointed place in the corner, or under
the side-board, and have had his biscuits and gravy
and bones once a day far from the fires and physical
comforts of his betters, but he had only one life and I
meant it to be a merry one even if it should be a month
or two the shorter. And yet he lived to fourteen, and
his end was worthy of him.

He was devoted to a cousin of mine who had a
big place near Bray in Co. Wicklow, where he could
hunt and enjoy himself, and we all three used to harry
the other cousins and their dogs from these head-
quarters. When I went to live in London for good, I
left him with him. When he was thirteen years old
(which was as near as we could get to his age, not
knowing the date of his birth), he became (apparently)
paralysed in his hind-quarters and my cousin felt that
it was not fair to him to keep him alive. He told me
that he put him in a dog-cart and drove him himself
to the vet in Bray. Half-way there he bent down to
him with the tears pouring down his face and said,
" Poor old Punch, I'll never see you any more," and
Punch got up on his four feet and walked round the
bottom of the cart, and they turned it round and drove
home again, and he lived for another year and died of
old age.

All our animals were people of character and had
the qualities beloved of children. We had a donkey
who had evidently once been in a circus, and used to
do all sorts of tricks to amuse us. I once heard yells

coming from the field at the back of the house and found my eldest son, aged about six, " held up " by the donkey, who was dancing all round him on his hind legs, showing off for all he was worth. He worshipped the pony and followed him like a dog, and when the latter died, he ran about the fields calling for him for weeks like a cow for her calf.

The pony was just as amusing as the donkey. He would allow one of the children to ride him, but not two at a time. It was purely a matter of dignity, for he could easily have carried three, but two he just kicked off. He had a very strong pride of race, and though he loved the donkey he refused to drive behind him in a tandem, and we had to give up this form of locomotion, for when he was in front he pulled the donkey off his feet. He was full of mischief. We had a governess cart and an old-fashioned small phaeton, and when he was in the latter he would go along splendidly for a while and then suddenly stop and turn round and look at us, and when he had had a good laugh would trot on again. It was rather alarming to nervous strangers who did not know him, but very amusing to us.

He, and the donkey, and the dogs and Pilot seemed to belong to one big happy family, and seemed to fit Hurstbourne better than Wyld's two horses. One of these was a Bolshevist and bit you whenever he saw you. The other was a crusted old Tory ; he was an admirable hunter once he got to the meet, but as he ran up the nearest bank every time he saw a motor-car he did not always turn up in time. He resented the advent of petrol in Hurstbourne Priors and kicked against the pricks of every hedge within miles at the mere smell of it.

But all our horses put together did not come up

to Wilkinson's " Lucy Bell." She was an old Siddeley four-seater, and a much older Communist than even Wyld's horse, inasmuch as she belonged to the original red-flag brigade. She was born somewhere about the time of the first Reform Bill, but, like all thoroughbreds, age could not wither her, and she never knew when she was beaten. She had her social ups and downs. She was at one time an aristocratic equipage, cushioned and glittering with nickel and varnish, and took the " quality " to pay calls ; thence she sank to the level of a freighter, with boards at the back to carry rows of cricketers. You could hear her snorts all over the village as she stood at the door with her engines running, and she trembled all over like a hunter outside a covert on the first day of cubbing.

She was one of the old school and let the Rolls-Royces pass her, it is true ; but she had been known to carry the whole Hurstbourne team of eleven heavy hilarious men to battle. Was she down-hearted ? Not a bit of it. She was running as well as ever for many a day after that, an aristocrat once more, painted and powdered, protesting occasionally, but polite and plucky as of old.

There was a race a few years ago, called " The Old Crocks' " race, over the London to Brighton course, and Lucy entered for it. Not only did she enter for it, but she won a gold medal for completing the distance with an hour and a half to spare !

There was no holding her after this, and when she heard that Wilkinson and I had an idea of going to Blagdon she pointed out that she could get us there by road in a quarter of the time it would take us by rail.

It was a memorable journey. As she was held together for the most part by string and catgut and odd bits of rope, it meant a stop at every other garage on

the way. The routine was always the same. As we
panted up to the filling-station a stillness would fall
upon the place. Then the man in charge would come
slowly out and gaze at her in a dream. He paid no
attention to orders—he seemed to be in a hypnotic
trance. The news seemed to travel telepathically, for
one by one the members of the staff would assemble
and stand there mute. Then there would be a murmur
or two and at the exact psychological moment when
their manners were going sky-high, one of us would
say :

"This is the old bird who won 'The Old
Crocks'' race to Brighton."

The effect was magical. In a moment they were all
over her like a swarm of bees. Nothing was too good
for her. They filled her up and polished her brasses ;
they blew up her tyres and tied on her lamps and re-
wired her brakes ; and when, with a triumphant snort,
she leapt off on her way, they cheered her out of sight.

She was not such a success as an economist. In the
time we took to get to Blagdon we might have done
the train journey there and back once or twice over.
But it was worth it. For sheer rapt attention on the
part of the public Lucy's front seat beat any concert
platform I ever was on.

XVIII

" IMPOSSIBLE " TROUT

ONE of the most case-hardened beliefs about the public singer is that he is a hot-house plant, utterly unable to face the everyday buffetings of the world, wrapped up to the eyes and sheltered from the winds of heaven and in a chronic state of acute catarrh. I knew a foreign violinist who travelled about with an agent, a secretary, an accompanist and a black servant, and who had to have the green-room warmed to a special temperature for the sake of his fiddle; but that certainly is not the way of the English singer, who is quite as good a rough-and-tumble sportsman as any of his countrymen. The conditions, however, which I personally prefer are certainly of the " hot-house " order. I like to sing in a room which is a blaze of light and packed from floor to ceiling, with every window tight shut, the air dense with tobacco and the temperature at about 200° Fahrenheit, and myself pouring with perspiration from every pore. It is easy to make things move in such conditions.

Therefore I loved the Bourne for her preference for a hot day. There used every now and then to be a phenomenal rise of fly in a north-easter, but as a rule the hotter the day the better the rise. A still, sweltering day on the chalk stream for me! To wake up in the morning and see the sun through the river mist and the trees dead still, and to know that the day is yours and that you will be hot the whole of it! I often lie awake and go over the old places in my mind. I come round the bend and see the fairy boats sailing down, and the great head-and-tailers, black against the white-blue water light, crossing and re-crossing, lazy and infinitely graceful. They are to me the very embodiment of " style," the perfection of motion with the greatest ease, the economy of visible effort which is the secret of all style whatever it be, in singing, or swimming or playing golf; in a Kreisler, a John Roberts, a kestrel, or a school of porpoises.

I do not know anything more beautiful in nature than the head-and-tailing trout. Why does not some enterprising cinema-nature-picture man give us the evening rise upon the " movies " ? It would hold its own against the cuckoo or the golden eagle. He would have to choose his day, when the evening light was pink upon the water and the black duns were sailing down thick, when the wave from each great shoulder rolled away in purple velvet and the widening rings overlapped and spent themselves. Let him first give us that perfect picture of evening peace among the poplars and the sedges and the golden mimulus ; and then, if he will, bring man upon the scene to spoil it all, and show us the whole battle of wits—the crawling to position, the casting of the little dun, the big nose coming up, the slow strike, the wild rush, the wearing-down, the netting, and the two-pounder on the bank.

I would infinitely rather fish to the rise than to visible fish. I love looking into the light on the water, watching for the rise, and seeing my fly float down into the ring, and never knowing till it comes to him whether he will take it or not. This is the chief charm of the evening rise at Stockbridge. You fish to the ring, and the tense excitement of watching it enter the circle and waiting for the strike is, for me, far greater than that of seeing any fish, however big, come to your fly. That was the only excitement, apart from the weather, that I missed on the Bourne, where, as I have before said, you could see your fish every time, watch every move he made, and almost follow the reasoning processes of trout in general as well as of your adversary in particular.

The Bourne taught me one thing which has been of infinite service to me whenever trout are visible, and that is, that you need never despair either of getting any rising fish that you do not actually put down, or—in shallow water—of bringing up a fish that apparently is not on the rise already.

The first of these is common enough. Everybody knows the insults he showers upon you, rushing to your fly, looking at it, and returning to the real article, sometimes coldly, sometimes with a flaunt of his tail; sailing up to it with a smile, and bumping it with his nose, knowing that he is making your heart jump into your mouth and your hand give a convulsive twitch; or opening his mouth at it and then suddenly turning round with a swirl as he spits it out; or, worst of all, following it right down to have a good look at it, while you grovel with your stomach on the ground and your head in the nettles and let the line go hang; and when at last you venture to look up, you find that he has deserted you long ago and is back again feeding at his old post. As long as he goes back again to the same spot and stays on top of the water, you are as likely to get him as not. It sometimes means a few minutes' rest and a change of fly, but as often as not you can wear down his patience without a change of any sort. There comes a moment, sooner or later, when he is either off his guard—generally immediately after taking the real fly—and takes yours in his stride, or when he will snap at it in sheer impatience as though he could not be bothered with the infernal thing any more.

There was a Longparish Common three-pounder who was a case in point. I was standing in the middle of the river directly behind him and could follow his temperamental impulses. I had risen him and missed him three times running, and he sulked at last ; but I knew he was a wearing-down case, and I stuck to him for nearly an hour without a change of fly. I decided finally to give him fifty more casts before leaving him —we deal in big figures in this process—and I got him on the fiftieth. I do not expect this to be believed.

But if you can wear a rising fish down you can also bring a non-rising fish up—by creating an artificial rise and persuading him that the duns have started in for the day. I have done it on the Bourne dozens of times, and was able once to demonstrate it to " Corrigeen " of the *Field*, who, though sceptical at first, accepted it at once when he saw it in performance. He has, I understand, practised it since himself with great success. Two things are necessary to bring it off—you must see your fish, and your sixth sense must tell you that he will rise if it is made worth his while. He may be lying motionless on the bottom, sullen and asleep to look at, he may not have a wag in his tail, he may, in fact, look hopeless for your purpose ; but if you know in your bones, as you do in some queer way, that he would be glad of a dun or two for breakfast, you can try for him with perfect confidence. One thing is sure —he is perfectly comfortable where he is, and is not going to trouble to come up unless it is really going to be a good thing—in other words, unless he is convinced that a rise has come on and is well set. What you have got to do is to persuade him that the river has never provided such a rise of dun in its existence,

and that if he does not come up for them he will have
missed the meal of a lifetime.

You keep pegging your fly above him, sometimes
in front of his nose, sometimes close to his right, sometimes to his left, sometimes far out in the circle and
sometimes at the back of his head. In fact, you must
cover the whole field of vision. There is no need to
change the fly ; the same one does for all. You may
do it a couple of hundred times before he will take
any notice. Then you will see an almost imperceptible
undulation of his body ; at the next cast his tail will
wag very slightly ; then he rises about two inches off
the bottom and settles back again ; then he either
rushes at the fly and takes it with a snap or, much
oftener, sails slowly up to it and starts quietly in on his
meal, fully believing that there is a good hour's feed
ahead of him. (The millionaire can, of course, send his
chauffeur up to the bridge above, with a box of flies,
and instructions to drop them one by one into the
various ripples. Why make a toil of a pleasure ?)

It is an almost invariable experience when duns
begin to come up after a long blank, that only the small
fish take them for the first few minutes. There is
evidently a reluctance on the part of their elders to
bestir themselves unless it means real business. The
" artificial " rise is simply a matter of patience and
keeping out of sight, and if the fish is worth it so is
the patience, and the watching of the progress of the
plot is as good as any " shocker."

I once had a visible encounter with a salmon. I
was fishing for bass in an estuary in Devonshire and
was standing on a rock which commanded a clear view
downstream, and was presently aware of a long dark
form following my sand-eel up towards me. As it
came near I saw it was a salmon. No salmon ever

received such affectionate attention. I joggled the bait in front of his eyes, I tickled his ribs with it, I blobbed it suddenly up against his nose, I swished it along his back and finally I tried to stroke-haul him. Anyhow, he sailed majestically up-river under my very feet, leaving me in a fury of self-recrimination at having somehow missed an obvious certainty.

A friend of mine had better luck. I was shooting in Scotland with the late Albert Vickers, and his son Billy, then a boy at Eton, got up early one morning and took a gun with him on the chance of a shot at a rabbit or some other beast in or out of season. The only thing he came across was a salmon sunning himself near the surface of a pool, and he promptly shot it. (The statute of limitations presumably holding good, I can give him away now.) When he produced it at breakfast his father gave him a sovereign for his early rising, casting, catching, and tailing, and Billy pocketed it, having miserably failed in the momentary struggle to tell the truth for once in his life. It was put right, however, in the evening, when his father broke one of his teeth on a pellet of shot.

I had an experience with a trout on the Kennet, which I always associate, quite undeservedly, with " snatching." It was in 1922, and I was staying with the late Mr. Giveen, who had taken the Mill fishing from Colonel Grove-Hills for the latter half of the season. His brother Charles and I had often stood on the bridge at the top, where the water falls down from the lake of Ramsbury Manor, and hungrily objurgated the great fat three-pounders which laughed at us from beneath. These were rovers by profession, and never stayed long enough in one place to be fished for individually from below, and were up to every trick from above. They would lie with their noses on the ledge

DRY FLY FISHING (!)

(This photograph was taken two days after the adventure, when the water had fallen about three feet)

immediately underneath us, and dreamily watch the smoke from our pipes ascending to the blue ; but the moment the top of a rod appeared over the edge, off they went. We tried concerted action many times, but as soon as ever one of the watchers disappeared from the bridge the pool was abandoned to two-year-olds. On this occasion I was passing by the sluice which forms a small side-carrier to the main fall and I put my head casually over the side, expecting nothing, and there, right below me, was a big golden trout tucked up under the boards, with his head down-stream and his tail up against the cracks where the water spurted through. He was doing no good there, so I felt it was my duty to get him.

It was an awful prospect. Immediately below him two planks ran across the sluice at intervals of about eight feet, and below them again in the fairway there was a veritable barricade of posts sticking up out of the stream in ragged profusion. There were three on the near side and two on the far side and a gaunt rubbing-post in the middle acting as a buoy, round which every sporting fish was in honour bound to double. Below these again there was another pole running right across the stream only four inches above the water, which swirled under it at a great pace. A more hopeless barbed-wire entanglement it would be hard to imagine to try and fish a fish out of, even if one hooked him. However, he was a beauty, and the fact that he was practically ungetable made it all the more exciting. I had up the ordinary tackle ; by all the laws of caution I should have put up a ginger-quill with a No. 1 hook and a Mayfly cast, but I reflected that if he got tangled up in the barriers a steel hawser would not hold him, and that if by some amazing fluke he ever came through, the fine tackle would be as good as anything else. Moreover, I should be able to swagger to the others about 4X casts and ooo hooks even more insupportably than before; so I stuck to what I had.

I stood well back where I could just see the tip of his nose, and he could not see me, reeled in the line to within six inches of the cast, and gently dropped the fly on to him. It was at once carried out by the stream. I thought it was going to be hopeless, when to my intense delight the back eddy swirled it round at exactly the right moment and brought it over him again. It was then seized once more by the stream and carried off afresh. The process was repeated automatically without my having to do a thing, and there went my fly playing " last across " with him, rushing up the backwater, tweaking his nose and dashing off down-stream before he could say a word. I was so delighted and laughing so hard that I could not help crawling up to see the fun, and I put my head over to have a look. He was intently absorbed in the game and never saw me. He appeared to take no notice at first and treated it all with dignified unconcern, but as the impudent little beast dashed past him smothering him with insults he began to get impatient, and I saw his tail detach itself from the sluice-board and begin to wag. Then he began to shake his head and bunch himself to attack. But nothing happened for a long time, and I was just going to give it up, as my arm was getting tired from the unnatural position, when I had a wonderful bit of luck. There was a twig sticking out from the wall on the far side over the back eddy, and the gut caught over it, and, before I knew it, there was the fly bobbing up and down in the water, right in front of him. This was too much. His enemy was delivered into his hands.

He leaped at it, seized it, knew in a moment what

had happened, and dashed off down-stream under the planks and through the posts and out into the pool at the bottom. There I had to leave him for a long time to settle himself, with my rod bent double under the first plank. Then the fun began. I cautiously passed it under this with one hand and retrieved it with the other, and did the same with the second plank. All idea of keeping the line taut was perforce abandoned. I still had the six upright posts and the flat pole beyond to negotiate. If he once got tangled up in these it would be all over. He was near the top of the pool now, and I lay flat on the ground with the point of the rod out in the space between me and the centre post, terrified lest he should swim up on the near side of A post, catch sight of me, and dash down on the far side or pay a visit to X, Y or Z post. I clung to Mother Earth like a tiger-skin on a polished oak floor. Sure enough, up he came. He swam through the near channel and roamed about under my eyes (or the corner of one of them) for about a fortnight apparently, and then swam slowly back to the pool the same way he had come !

It was almost too good to be true ! But the crux was still to be faced—there was still the flat pole to get under. It ran across the top of the pool, with a space of about four inches between it and the water. It was a bare two inches thick and it was quite rotten. I had to get the rod under it somehow (for I could never risk letting him out of the pool again), and I could only just reach it with my hand by holding on to the bank above with my toes and descending apoplectically towards the water. It crackled loudly the moment I touched it. I had to lean hard on the horrible thing with my right hand, pass the rod under with my left, scrabble it out again somehow with my right on

N

the other side, change hands and work myself back up the bank. It groaned and shivered its timbers and fired off shots like a machine-gun—but the little iron-blue had squared it and it held. It was not all over even then, for if the fish had caught sight of me he would have dashed up through the uprights again ; so I backed slowly out of sight into a withy-bed and stayed there till there was not a kick left in him. As a matter of fact, he had done it all for me by returning through the posts the same way he had come. The only credit I can take is for keeping out of sight and performing gymnastics with an almost superhuman skill for one of my size and weight. He weighed 2¼ lbs.

I am reminded by this of another " snatching " experience in which I only played a minor part. My Ceylon brother Geoffrey and I were staying at Wilton. It was a really hot day—another of the few I ever remember in England—and a Sunday. Sunday fishing was forbidden at Wilton, but there was no definite rule against poaching. In the course of our wanderings he and I had discovered an old cannibal who lived under one of the small bridges. His size was immeasurable, for only his head and shoulders were visible ; the rest of him faded away in the darkness of the bridge. He lived, so far as we could see, on pound trout, dabchicks, field-mice and the superfluous kittens of the Wylye valley. Anyhow, he was a permanent menace to the fishing, and better out of the water than in it.

We found an old bow with which the children had slain their enemies in their early days. There were still a couple of feet of the old string dangling from one end of it. On to this we lashed a Mayfly cast and on to that a large fat yellow Mayfly. Fishing on Sundays being forbidden and the prospects of success being anyhow nebulous, we did not take a landing-net. We stole off to the bridge and we tossed up as to who should do the fishing and who should be ghillie, and Geoffrey won. The bridge had no parapet, so he lay flat on his stomach, poked the end of the bow over the edge and dropped the Mayfly on to the water.

Meanwhile I had crawled out on to the bank above and taken up position as watcher. The arrangement was that he was to manœuvre the end of the " rod " into the right position under my directions, and then " blob " the Mayfly up and down over Hannibal's nose, and at the inevitable moment, when his power of resistance would suddenly collapse, I was to yell and he was to strike.

It was a longer business than we had fondly imagined. Hannibal was a bad audience. The moment my face appeared upon the platform he made for the door. We waited for what seemed weeks, grovelling among the ants and perspiring in the baking heat. We were convinced that all was over when he suddenly reappeared. What happened then proved to me once and for all that where food is concerned the oldest trout is as little able to resist temptation as the youngest child. For a solid hour we rose him and missed him. After each bungle he would lie at the bottom for a full ten minutes and then would wriggle up to the top again and have another snap at the fly. I would yell, my brother would strike, there would be a mighty commotion and off he would go into the bowels of the bridge, only to reappear presently and take up his old quarters immediately underneath the Mayfly.

But we got him in the end, though it was no fault of ours. He suddenly shot up from below, seized the fly in a fury before I had time to shout, and dashed off with it, and in a second Geoffrey was rolling about on the ground with the bow bent almost double over the edge of the bridge. It was exactly like Nanook and the seal. My brother was 6 ft. 6 in., and at one time his body was curved like a crescent moon, with his toes dug into the earth above and his head up the archway below, and at another he was stretched out like a high diver. I was waiting greedily for the moment when he would be pulled over the top, but, as a matter of fact, it was the other way about; for when he had played him to a standstill, I reached down to tail him and, as usual, fell headlong into the river.

In view of this, and the riddance of bad rubbish, all was forgiven when we turned up with him, and we were looked upon rather as heroes than otherwise. He was about three feet long and weighed 2¾ lbs., and with a cloth over his head might easily have passed for a conger-eel.

I had a bitter pill to swallow in the evening of the aforesaid day on the Kennet. There had not been any rise, it was blowing half a gale in my face and I was walking disconsolately home, when I saw a ring under the far bank. I threw a fly as near to the spot as I could see in the gloom and to my surprise found as I tightened up that the fish was on. He did not dart for the bulrushes as I expected, but swam slowly up and down in mid-stream. I thought he must be a little one, but suddenly I caught a glimpse of him and my knees knocked. He was a giant. Never was anybody more gently shepherded. He was guided by wireless. Neither of us made any fuss. I must have been invisible on the bank, but it was the bank alas! that did it; I could not expect to get the better of two high banks in one day. Once more I lay on my stomach, and I felt for him with the net. It was a big net, and he stretched right across it. I could not reach far enough out to get him fairly into the middle of it, and I did not dare to pull him hard with the fine tackle I had on. Three times I got him to the net and three times I boggled him, and in the end he gently broke away as the current was bringing him into the bank. Of course, he was the biggest fish of the season ; I saw him once quite plainly. But he proved once more that keeping out of sight is the key to success, though it did not quite unlock the door on this occasion. I had him on for more than ten minutes, and during all that time he never made a rush or a splash or any protest whatever.

It is hard to analyse one's emotions on occasions such as these, when the fish of one's dreams is snatched, as it were, out of its glass case. One's first impulse is to sit down and cry, but, having left such remedies behind with one's youth, one turns naturally to invective. And, here again, there is a difficulty. The same medicine is really not adequate for such varied ills as flies caught in the back of one's coat, barbed wire on one's waders, water in one's boots, a be-trampled landing-net, and all the rest. Personally, utterance having failed, I become possessed of a dumb and benumbed energy. I pick up the routine of the day, wind in the line, examine the fly, light a cigarette, and walk slowly off into the blue, conscious only that something has stopped inside and that the wheels of articulate emotion have ceased working. Tragedy is supposed to stun, and that is my experience. I make up for it later.

XIX

THE KENNET

THIS particular part of the Kennet has every-thing that the dry-fly fisherman wants. It runs slow, it is true, as the Kennet does, but it is deep and full of fish in condition. It is never re-stocked and is a testimony to the wisdom of that policy, for every fish is a wild fish and beautiful to look at, long and deep and pink as a salmon, and as far as numbers go they are apparently inexhaustible. You may think at the end of a week that you know every fish in the place, and his position, and next day there will be a dozen or two more showing up in fresh places, pushing out great waves in the evening rise. You may walk along the water one day and think that they have deserted the river, and yet if you watch closely you will see a ring come creeping out from under the near bank, and another, maybe, farther up, and another and another.

Then your difficulties begin. There is generally a north-west wind waiting to blow your fly into the sedges above his head; and even when it does go straight and your iron-blue floats safely down the little channel you feel as lonely as a lost dog. There has been no rise to tune you up, and you are almost afraid that he will take your fly. These are the occasions when you snap your fly off in his mouth.

These Kennet fish are well educated by August, and know the look of a cast so well that they will often just ignore your fly and go on feeding on the genuine article. There was one two-pounder in the Mill water at Ramsbury who fed consistently from morning to night for a whole season without ever making a slip or even pausing to congratulate himself.

I remember another fish on Chalkley's water at Winchester which enjoyed itself in very much the same way. I was playing cricket for Hurstbourne against the 2nd XI of the School, and wandered off to see one of the boys fishing. At this particular time they were allowed to fish, and were even provided with a keeper to coach them. This boy had the expert at his elbow, but he was quite superfluous, for I never want to see anyone throw a better fly. The fish he was trying for was having the time of his life. There was a big hatch of dun and he was rising like mad. Half a dozen would come floating over him with the boy's in the middle; he would take the right and left and leave the other alone. He would take one in front and one behind, and let the artificial one go by. Occasionally you would see him heave towards it, and your heart would jump into your mouth, but he used just to knock it out of the way with his nose and then gulp down another within an inch of it. I am convinced that he saw the joke of it and was enjoying himself far more than the boy.

A Variant is about the best all-round evening fly for the part of the Kennet that I have described, but it is no good until it begins to grow dark. You may try it, say, at 8.30, and put down every fish you cast for, and at 8.40 they may come to it at once.

I like the Variant, too, because—in spite of its vagaries at sundown—it is as much a day fly as a night fly, and I feel proportionately less a criminal; for as I said before, I can never get away from the feeling that the " big fly and the stout cast " night-fishing is more or less murder. The big red sedge in the dark on the Kennet is bad enough, but at least a fish can make a dash for the weeds and perhaps keep your fly as a memento. A trout who is firmly hooked on the " fuzzy-buzzy " and the Mayfly cast at Blagdon ought not to have a dog's chance. Evening fish are feeding too passionately to be on their guard, and it is too dark to see the gut, and when once he is fairly hooked the tackle never gives him a look-in.

Still one does it, though if one analysed one's sensations one would find that it is the lust of size, of poundage, rather than the joy of battle which is in one's mind. I ease my own particular conscience by easing the check of my reel to its easiest and letting him run as far out into the lake as he will—the farther the better. There is a certain grossness about the whole business far removed from the refinement of the diminutive fly and the fine point dropped in the eye of the sun and the teeth of the wind on to the little patch between the weed-beds, or under the flags on the near side, or into the little bay in the far bank on the off-chance that the infinitesimal moment before it drags may be the one moment for him. These criticisms only refer to night-fishing ; in the day-time Blagdon is as fine and fair as any Scottish loch. But, whenever I get a fish at night on a big fly and a thick cast I think of Krag the Kootenay ram.

This does not apply, I need hardly say, to the evening rise on the river. The hour at sundown on the Kennet is the most difficult fishing I know, owing to the ultra-visibility at the moment and the Brobdingnagian proportions which one apparently assumes in that particular light. The evening rise brings out all the vacillation, cowardice, impatience, despair and vituperation which civilisation pretends to have

conquered in the man-animal. The mere sight of the
shoal of hump-backed whales sets your knees shaking
and your stomach quaking and your teeth grinding,
and makes you feel like the spaniel who has got to the
three dinners before the other two. There never yet
was a fisherman born who was not beset by the temptation to leave the fish he is trying for for the one just
beyond him. The near one has let the fly go by a couple
of times, maybe, or has risen and missed once, and
instinctively you shift to the new one so as not to
waste the precious minutes of the dusk, and before
you know it the rot has set in.

You begin whipping your fly deliriously and bang
it down with a splash, you wind the line round your
rod or catch the hook in the cast, you put your hand
into the nettles or slip into the water over your waders
and scare every fish within distance ; or when you do
get a rise you give a lightning strike, see a boil in the
water and find the point is gone. My experience is
that when you have picked your fish it is better to stick
to him until you find for certain that he is no use.
Eliminate all the others from your mind in the meantime. You never know that a forward movement may
not startle the trout nearest to you and send him
flying up-stream, and suddenly the pool that was a-boil
may be as still as a dew pond.

In most rivers you know the big fish and their evening feeding-places, but in the Kennet fresh ones appear
in new places when the sun goes down, and you have
just got to watch the wave and judge the size of the
shoulder behind it or pick out the big head-and-tailer
against the light.

The big " head-and-tailer trout," whose praises I
sang earlier, is about the most exciting beast that swims.
His very deliberation and monumental calm give you

a feeling of physical inferiority. Up comes his nose and down again and then at a long interval—an agonisingly long interval—up comes his tail about three feet away, and down again, and up comes your heart into your mouth and down again at the awful thought of having to cast at a man-eater and of what will happen if you miss him. On such occasions everything depends upon how you strike. When he is feeding unsuspectingly he is just as likely to take your dun as another, but woe betide you if you strike too quick. The bigger he is the bigger his mouth, comparatively speaking, and the slower he moves the more deliberate he is in opening and shutting it. After all he is in no hurry. He is by *force majeure* master of his beat, and is not obliged to snap at unconsidered trifles, and he is much too much of a gentleman to call your attention to the way he eats his dinner. So he cruises about, lazily opening his jaws and letting the flies float in. Whip your fly up quickly and you have whipped it out of them before he has had time to close them, and there is a boil and a prodigious splash and he is off, scattering the other candidates far and wide, and that particular pool is spoiled for the evening.

The " sticklebacker " at Blagdon is exactly the same, and exactly the opposite. There is no quiet about him. He rushes at your fly like lightning ; but he rushes at it with his mouth open. You have got to give him time to take it and close his mouth on it, and then strike for all you're worth. It requires an almost superhuman power of control, for that wild dart of the big fish is enough to unbalance any mind.

The river evening head-and-tailer is about the slowest " strike " there is. He has not the wolf-breed habits of the Blagdon hunter. Just a slow raising of the right arm with the line held lightly in the fingers of the left hand ; he will see to the rest. And the fun is only beginning then. Your one object is to get him down-stream without queering the pitch ahead of you. If you jump to your feet anything may happen. Your only chance is to keep out of sight, for " out of sight " means " out of weeds." The big fish I lost on the Kennet, of which I spoke above, was a case in point. There were a dozen weed-beds and bulrush groves into which he could have dashed, and would have dashed if he had seen me, but he was content to swim up and down the fairway till he was done.

Every fish, as a rule, makes a bolt for cover when first hooked ; but if you can get him out of it the first time you can probably head off all his other efforts—provided you do not show yourself. Once he sees the man on the bank it is hell-for-leather to the end. Some modern Haydn should write an ode to, or rather a dirge on, " the impatient landing-net."

The fish I love to play is the fellow who bores down deep and never shows upon the surface. You follow his course by the line cutting through the water with never a sign of the cast—he is much too deep for that ; the fish who takes charge and pulls heavy like a salmon and tells the reel what he wants. The authority of his pull is the only index to his size, and you cannot tell whether he is two pounds or four until the last moment. He is far less showy than the star performer who dashes off up-stream for thirty yards with the reel screaming. This is exciting enough, but a little fish can do it just as noisily as a big one. The " strong silent man " for me every time, with the salmon " chug-chug " on the line, and the steady strain and occasional sweep from the straight, and the mysterious masterful sense of reserves !

There is a little tributary of the Kennet, which runs

in half a mile below Ramsbury, called the Whittonditch, which contained (in 1914) just such powerful fish. It is the most ridiculous apology for a river ever seen, about ten feet across in most parts, and not much more than half a mile long in the fishable part. It belonged in those days to Mr. Rennie and Mr. Lee, and they gave me several days on it. I am bound to say that I was sceptical about its capabilities when I first saw it, but I very soon repented of my unbelief.

As was the case with the Bourne, its length depended on the amount of rain in the winter, and its proprietors often had to collect odd fish which had wriggled miles up the valley and put them back into the half-mile at the bottom where the springs did not dry up. When I think of that absurd little carrier and the great trout that used to bore through its depths like submarines, I can only wonder at the cheek of trying to tackle them at all.

I love the Kennet and everything to do with it, and apparently it loves me, judging from the number of times it has taken me into its embrace, its only rival in this respect being the Spey. But despite its brown colour it is eminently sanitary and I have no complaints to make. It has always treated me royally. I can never remember a day on that water, from Littlecote up, when there has not been a rise at some time, and whenever I have failed it has been through no ill-will on its part. Two days which I had on the Littlecote water one September are conspicuous examples of how it treated me. On the first of these I got four brace of fish weighing 9¾ lbs., and on the second six brace weighing 15¾ lbs. But just to sit and smoke a pipe in the meadows by the orchards of Ramsbury (which ceased to be a bishopric in 1000 A.D.) is good enough for me, if I never see a fish all day.

And what of Hurstbourne Priors?* Is it less beautiful, less old, than Ramsbury? The Romans lived there before the Saxon invasion. (A denarius of the reign of Gordian, 248 A.D., was dug up not long ago at New Barn close by.) It is called Hissaburna in the Saxon charters of the eighth century; in the eleventh century we find Eisseburn, its name in the Domesday Book; in the twelfth century Hesseburna Priors; Hussiborne in the fourteenth century; and finally Hurstbourne Priors in the sixteenth century. And, save for one brief lapse when Dorothy Wallop in 1682 gave the " silver paten to ye Church of Down Husband " (which is still used), Hurstbourne Priors it has remained to this day.

On the occasion of which I spoke earlier, when I got over the wire cattle-fence and crept up under the trees below the cascade, I was as much in another world as I can ever be in this one. I stood in the midst of great mortared stones, green with age, the foundations of " the fayre old house " which Sir Robert Oxenbridge bought in 1558. He died in 1574, and his canopied tomb is in the North Wall of the church. I wonder if he was a better Englishman than the seven young men whose memorial hangs on the wall a dozen feet away from him. They were killed in the Great War.

The bells that tolled for them must have tolled for many wars before theirs. Here is their message, divinely sweet as I can testify:

The first (Ellis and Henry Wright, 1667), says:

> " I, as treble surge."

The second: " I, as second sing."
The third: " I, as third ring."

* I am indebted for these particulars to a delightful lecture, " Hurstbourne in old and modern times," by Mr. J. Carbery Evans.

The fourth :   " I, as fourth sound."
The fifth :   " I, as tenor hum around."
The sixth :   " Now the tenor is by Henry Bagley, 1741.
               I to the church the living call,
               And I to the grave summon all.
               Attend the instruction which I give
               That so you may forever live."

I love to think that the little Bourne, who talked to
me of snipe and swifts and sedge-warblers and silver
trout and iron-blues, was running there a thousand
years ago, and that at Chapmansford (the " cheap-
dealer's crossing ") the Romans stopped to water their
horses within a yard or two of the spot where I caught
the three trout on August 29th, 1904. In the very
meadow where we had the flower-show and ran sack-
races and rode in the merry-go-rounds, the archers and
Morris-dancers and " Chimney-sweeps " held their
sports in the days of Henry VIII. And the big yew
tree, which Herbert Baverstock and his six comrades
knew so well in their short lives, was standing in that
churchyard 400 years before Sir Robert Oxenbridge
was born.

XX

FISHING, SINGING AND POACHING

WE left Hurstbourne Priors early in 1913. Our second son was growing at a prodigious rate—far too quickly for his good—and the doctor said that we ought to leave the river valley and go to higher ground. We found a house on top of the ridge above Hungerford, some 600 feet above sea-level, and there we went to live. It did all we hoped it would do for him, and I am thankful that we went there, but the old village and the old life were gone for good, and I and the little river that was my friend had said good-bye. I often go to see her still, and I sit beside her on the bank and we talk of old times, but we both know that those happy days can never come again.

I wish some poet would write an epic of the Hampshire Bourne. He would have to be a fisherman himself—" Fischer und Poet dazu "—for a little learning is a dangerous thing, especially in sport. A song was sent to one of our famous singers a little while ago, the refrain of which ran as follows :

> " Hurrah ! for the girls who follow the fox
> While the dogs come barking behind."

This is somewhat similar to the criticism of a concert which appeared in a North of Ireland paper :

" The Rev. Mr. Moriarty gave a fine rendering of Chopin's ballad in a flat, and in ' Kathleen Mavourneen ' Miss Maguire undoubtedly made grand use of her tonsils."

Perhaps the poets are more cautious than the novelists whose heroines speak with a " deep throaty contralto " (an appalling combination) and sing the Choral Symphony as a duet after dinner. They play chords on the organ but they leave fly-fishing and singing unsung.

There are a few fishing songs in *The Compleat Angler*, and there is, of course, *Die Forelle* (The Trout) of Schubert to represent the two branches of song, but the latter is not one of the best of Schubert's Lieder. It has obtained a fictitious value simply, I feel sure, because it is about the only song in existence which deals with the chase of the river-fish. It is far more beautiful in its instrumental form, used as the subject of the D major quintet. Perhaps the composer felt that the actual music did not fit the song but was too good to be lost ; or perhaps he did not approve of muddying a stream to catch a trout that was too clever for him in clear water.

There are hundreds of songs dealing with the men who go down to the sea in ships, from shanties and folk-songs to ballads about nets and herrings, but never, so far as I know, an ode to the salmon or the trout or the grayling or to the man on the bank who is after them, with the exception of " The Angler's Song " (Henry Lawes, 1595), and another " Angler's Song " by the late Sir Charles Stanford.

If any man could have set such an epic to music it would have been the last-named, for not only was he a fisherman himself, but in his setting of Moira O'Neill's immortal *Fairy Lough* he has left us the most beautiful idyll of fresh water ever written.

Perhaps he remembered too well his experience on a Scottish loch with Francis Harford. The weather had been spotless. The heavens were as brass. There had not been a cloud in the sky or a fish in the water for a fortnight. They played " patience," and waited for the dawn. Suddenly one evening Harford leapt to his feet and said he was going out. He felt in his bones, he said, that the fish were going to come up. Stanford withered him. He read him out the menu of the dinner and drew amusing comparisons between the gourmand filling himself full in the dining-room and the poor devil flogging the empty water from the boat, and finally bade farewell to him on the steps with jeers.

In two hours Harford was back. Stanford was again standing on the steps smoking his pipe and bursting with humorous remarks that he had thought of at dinner. As Harford came near he appeared to be carrying a corpse over his shoulders. When he came closer Stanford saw that his waders were hanging down in front and that he had what looked like a hump on his back.

" Well, my boy," he said, " have you got those fish in your bones ? "

" No," said Harford, " I've got them in my bags," and he unwound the waders from round his neck, pulled the string at the top and tumbled out on to the ground four trout weighing 18¾ lbs. !

There is also a song called " Salutation," by Joseph Holbrooke, a setting of a Whitman-esque poem by an American writer, which graphically describes my own feelings when I have turned a corner and found another party at lunch on my pet beat :

> " O generation of the thoroughly smug and thoroughly
>   uncomfortable,
> I have seen fishermen picnicking in the sun,
>   . . . their smiles full of teeth, and heard ungainly
>   laughter."

o

The poet must have tried to speak to a competitor during an angling contest.

To me Vaughan Williams's *Silent Noon* (Rossetti) is lived in the wild mint and yellow irises of the water-meadows, with the swifts and the sand-martins in the chalk-scollops, and the drumming snipe and the dragon-flies. Whenever I sing it I wander off in dreams to one such spot in the Test valley.

But landing-nets and waders ! Muddyings of the crystal stream as crude as *Die Forelle* ! I have lain on my back countless times " in the long fresh grass," with my rod stuck into the ground at my side and my head on my fishing-bag, and lived through Brahms's *Feldeinsamkeit*, and watched the white clouds brushing across the enfolding blue and felt as though I " long were dead and borne along to Heaven."

There are songs in hundreds of the brook and the meadow and even of the birds, from the skylark to the nightingale. Let some old-fashioned Victorian fisherman who has been brought up on the " flexible tiger " and the " sinuous worm " of Haydn's *Creation* take a look at Ravel's *Martin-pêcheur* (The Kingfisher). He will probably abandon kingfishers *et hoc genus omne* in a hurry. And yet, strange to say, with all its barbaric harmonies and quasi-impossible melodic intervals, it gives a real impression of the hypnotic suspense which held the fisherman fascinated and the rod immovable.

Schubert was one of the few great composers who felt the poem of the river. The *Schöne Müllerin* is an epic of the mill-stream, and yet neither poet nor composer gave a thought to the trout that lived in it. I own it would be hard to compose, 'or sing, a song about dry-fly fishing—even about the fiftieth cast ! In Schubert's day the worm and the muddied water were about the limits of the horizon, and even in my

day in Germany the native was a primitive performer ;
(Ravel's fisherman, too, by all the signs, aspired no
higher than the float), and it is a far cry from *Die
Forelle* to the sherry-spinner and the tup and the
orange-quill.

I prophesied some years ago in a lecture at the Royal
Society of Arts that in the course of progress [*sic*] and
the search for the *aliquid novi* the human voice with its
priceless gift of speech, the holy gift which makes it
unique among musical instruments in its power of
direct appeal through words to the human emotions,
would one day be dragged from its high estate and
used as a mere colour-instrument of the band.

That day has arrived. The great composers of the
preceding generations have practically exhausted the
possibilities of legitimate orchestration, the bleating of
stopped brass is already *passé*, and the bedizenings of
Bach with tambourines and harp-glissandos have come
off second best in the competition with the banjo and
the sobbing saxophone. But youth had to be served,
and something new served up ; so they shanghaied
the singer. They did not stop to reason what were his
functions and his limitations, or what a poor figure
he would cut beside the clarinets and oboes. If you
had asked them for a loan of their Labrador to kill
your rick-rats, they would have sarcastically referred
you to a wire-haired terrier ; if you had borrowed one
of their thoroughbreds to mow your lawn they would
have sent for the police and an Inspector of the
R.S.P.C.A. But experiment keeps a blind eye for analo-
gies ; there was still the singer to operate upon. So
you can see the poor devil now any day standing in the
orchestra, a Samson shorn of his locks, yawping like a
cat on the tiles, and blushing from head to foot before
the fidgeting audience ; while his immortal voice,

stripped of its language, cowers naked and ashamed, emasculated, an apology for an instrument, piping out empty vowel-sounds without beauty, poetry or manhood.

" Blest pair of Sirens, pledges of Heaven's joy,
  Sphere-born harmonious sisters, Voice and Verse."

Milton was wiser than he knew. Of course, this philippic must not be taken too seriously ; but there's many a true word spoken in jest. There are signs to-day that it has outstayed its welcome.

I look forward likewise to the day when the dry-fly fisherman will press the button and find all the rest done for him. The profiteer millionaire, sitting in his smoking-room, will be informed by hydrophone that the fish are moving in the Saw-mill meadow ; the hydroscope will show him that the iron-blue is up ; the Rolls-Royce will take him to the cow-gate ; the theodolite (fixed to the butt) will give him the angle of Slippery Sam's rise ; a press on button No. 1 will ejaculate the fly on to the top of Sam's head ; button No. 2 will regulate the strike, wind him in automatically and play him to a standstill ; and the ghillie does the rest. Or, if he is a bottom-fisher, he can go to sleep on the bank or in the boat, with his head upon the champagne basket, until the electric bell rings and the blue light tells him he has hooked a dace, or the orange light a dab, or the red light (with explosions) a conger-eel.

As a matter of fact an initial experiment was partially made at Blagdon. An American turned up one day with fool-proof tackle and a rod to which he had fixed an automatic self-winding reel. In due course of time he hooked a fish and pressed the button, and the next thing he knew was a five-pound trout glaring at him through the ring at the end of his rod.

There is no reason why the ballad of the conger, caught on a fly-rod (foul-hooked if you like), should not be as exciting as Schubert's *Erlking*. The idea was already anticipated in an American newspaper which announced that I was going to sing " The Eel-ring " (= The Erl-King) by Schubert, together with " The Lands of Ice " (= " The Sands of Dee "), and " The Heavy Cow " (= " The Kerry Cow "). I believe it was the same paper which expressed the feelings of its readers by advertising my song-recitals as " Mr. Plunket Greene's long recitals."

The poacher used to give the poet a chance. He had his romantic side, as I know from experience ; but the Mills bomb has rather taken the poetry out of it, and, like the composers, we march with the times—or as far in front as we can get when bombs are expected.

There are many mill-pools I should like to explore with a hand-grenade, purely for purposes of research. There is hardly a mill-pool in the country that has not got its Fafner or some other mythical monster hiding in its depths, but even in Mayfly time I have never seen a glimpse of his tail, and I sometimes wonder whether mill-pools are not a fraud. You get an occasional good fish in the evening at the foot, in the shallows, but the back eddies where the big ones should lie generally seem empty. And yet in those deep waters there must occasionally be giants. What would that water-quake reveal ? Should we see Kipling's two sea-serpents, blind maybe, tossed up into the sunlight for the first time since they found " the better 'ole," or just a spray of yearlings and half-pounders ? I would put my money on the latter.

I suppose it is wrong to have an admiration for a criminal, but there was one poacher to whom I take off my hat. The brother of a friend of mine had been looking out for some fishing, and one day he saw an advertisement in a daily paper to say that there was a stretch of four miles of excellent water not far from London to be let for the season for £150, application to be made to Mr. Blank at a given address. He met Mr. Blank by appointment, and the latter begged him not to buy a pig in a poke, but to go down with him and have a day on the water before committing himself. He very naturally agreed. It was lovely weather. The fish were rising, and they were big and strong and plenty. He made a good bag and was delighted with himself and the fishing, and gave Mr. Blank a cheque on the spot.

He and his friends had fine sport there for a month or two, and then one day, while he was stalking his favourite fish, an old gentleman came up to him and said :

" I'm afraid, sir, you've made a mistake. This is private water."

" Oh, no," he said, " I've taken it for the season."

" The devil you have ! " said the old gentleman. " Unfortunately it belongs to me and I haven't let it."

Then it all came out. Mr. Blank knew the fishing and knew that it was not keepered, and had taken his chances. No doubt he had had many a pleasant day there himself, before sacrificing it for £150. He deserved the money anyhow ; and in the end the other man got his money's worth, too, for the landlord said he was not going to see him let down, and gave him the run of the water until the end of the season, like the fine old sportsman he was.

The poaching instinct is latent in us all, and is only held in check by our public school training. There was a river in Hertfordshire which was rather like the Irish bog of which the local poacher said :

" Is it shnipes you mean, sir ? See here, sir, don't you go into that bog widout your gun or begob they'd ate you ! "

It had a series of artificial dams and the trout were literally jostling one another under them. I could see their big backs heaving out of the water, and they were quite oblivious of my presence. They stonily refused every fly, and the temptation to cast a big sedge into the brown of them and pull something out by main force was almost irresistible. But fortunately I waited for the evening rise and got eleven fish and remained *preux chevalier*.

I once poached a conger-eel in Mullaghmore harbour on the far west coast of Sligo when I was a schoolboy. I call it poaching because I did not fish for him. I stuck him with a fork on the end of a pole. I was sorry I did, for he towed me and the boat about a hundred yards out to sea before he twisted the fork out of the handle and went off.

I remember with shame other crimes which I perpetrated there. I used to give bread soaked in sherry to the ducks and chickens in the farmyard. The ducks were absolutely human in the way they groped for equilibrium, but the hens fought like cats. There was a gannet which we had picked up on the shore with a broken wing, and to which we had given the run of the farmyard. He refused the sherry and bitters, but made up for it by suddenly swallowing a live sparrow which, owing to circumstances over which he had no control, was, in the Sligo euphemism, " not very shtrong on his feet."

Retribution fell upon me swiftly. The only time in my life that I was " the worse for drink " was one early morning at Mullaghmore. (I am sorry to shatter the encrusted popular belief that all public performers are

drunkards and end their days in a home for inebri-
ates.) I had been out with the mackerel boats since
5 a.m., and got back some hours later starved and
chilled to the bone. A friendly sailor gave me a glass
of poteen to warm me, and in the light of my subsequent experiences I left the chickens alone after that.

We had a cousin, A. D. Greene, the Oxford
cricketer, staying with us there. His father (affection-
ately known in Clifton as " College Greene ") was a
great entomologist and had a famous collection of
butterflies. One night a big moth flew in at our
window at Mullaghmore, and my mother caught it
and handed it over to my cousin. I do not know how
much he knew about moths, but his fisherman's sixth
sense told him it was something out of the common.
He set it up on a fishing-net cork and sent it to his
father. It turned out to be a *Chærocampa celerio* (Sphingi-
dæ), which had never been seen in Ireland before, and
of which only a few specimens had ever previously
been taken in the British Isles. The larvæ feed on
vines, and there were no vines within miles of
us !

That place was a heaven for a schoolboy in those
happy old Irish days. We sailed and fished and shot
blue rock pigeons from the caves, balanced in a boat
on an Atlantic roller, and rowed and swam with
nothing between us and America. But this was on
the black cliffs of far Sligo, and we are farther than
ever away from the Bourne.

And yet not so far. I had a dream not long ago
which linked the two. I was lying in the old familiar
spot at the foot of the water where the three rivers
meet, and was smoking and watching the sand-martins
in the white chalk scollop under the yews. A sedge-
warbler was talking to me in a bush close by, the swifts

were swooping round my head, and the water-rats were burrowing in and out of the weed-beds. The ground was yellow with irises and smelt of wild mint, and the sky was blue as sapphire. As I looked I saw that the big Longparish Common fish were slowly swimming through the wire and taking up position one by one above the weed-patches in the streams on either side of me as if to challenge me to battle. And just then a black cocker-spaniel came through the sedges on my left. He took no notice of me, but just trotted about snuffing and hunting. He did this for a long time, and then he suddenly came and sat down beside me without saying a word, and we looked at the river together; and presently he leaned over against me and put his head on my shoulder, and in a moment I was back again in Ireland, a little boy going back to school across the Channel, and I was sitting on the old seat in the garden that knew those tears so well, and my own old dog was leaning up against me as he used to do with his head on my shoulder and snuffing through his nose to tell me he understood, and the Kingstown boat somehow sailed from Mullaghmore !

Surely, of all the pains which mortal has to suffer, nostalgia is the worst. There is nothing in after life to equal the pangs of home-sickness as a boy, far worse for every league of sea between. I do not believe that I have ever got over it altogether or left it behind with my youth. I feel it with the Bourne and I like to think she feels it, too, and that she sent me the black spaniel to tell me to come back.

The hedges along the Whitchurch road bristle with telegraph wires ; motors pour across the Beehive bridge in a never-ending stream ; cycles and side-cars blare their horns and dash by with straining eyes ; they look not to the right or left but, like wild-geese,

hurry to their destination. But when I go to see her I
step off the highway at the bridge among the red and
white cows and the snipe and the kingfishers into her
peaceful village.

No enterprising newspaper has sent a war-corre-
spondent to discover it as yet. The tripper has not
found it out. The people in the big house have kept
it sacred from the charabanc and the jerry-builder
and the bungalow. It lies there, leaning against the
shoulder of the park, untouched, remote and unassail-
able as a Scottish deer-forest. But the silver trout are
gone.

In the last sentence is contained what I have called
the tragedy of the Bourne. The Test trout is the king
of all the river trout. He is as far above his neighbour
as the English partridge is above the " Frenchman."
Thoroughbred, beautiful, careless, pugnacious, sporting, English, clean and affectionate, he loved the
Bourne as his mother. It is for him she mourns, for
she loved him as her son. We starved him to death.
And when he was no more and the fear of his prowess
had died away, the yellow strangers crept up under
the banks, in spies first and then in battalions, and
stole his birthright.

Let no one think that the Bourne herself is dead.
Above the viaduct, it is true, her day is past. One afternoon in January (1924) I walked to the upper beat of
the old fishing. From the pollard to the upper end is
a short half-mile of what should be the finest spawning
water in England. There was not a minnow to be seen.
I wonder how many great trout, urged up-stream each
autumn by the call of nature, have strayed into the
mazes of the graveyard below and disappeared for
good. I stood within a dozen yards of the spot where
I had caught the 3¾-pounder in 1903, and searched the

golden gravel, in dumb despair, for some sign of remembrance. Alas! poor Yorick! It grinned at me pathetically like some yellow skull.

But you can walk through the meadows on either side of the Whitchurch road and see enough fish to last you for a lifetime; fish, too, that it will take you all your time to master. (I got 2½ brace one day in August (1923), within a hundred yards of the Beehive bridge, and was mighty proud of it.) Walk up to the cascade and you will find the water fuller of them than ever before. The " time-wasters " cruise in the broad water as of old, and there is a four-pounder, the station-master tells me, under the iron bridge. But they are not her children; hers perished in the famine.

Let me say once more that the owners were never to blame. We were supposed to know. They did what we asked them to do, and when the bad times came they said no word of reproach, though the Bourne was even more to them than to us. But that was not their only danger.

XXI

THE FUTURE OF THE BOURNE[*]

I WENT to Hurstbourne Priors that day in August 1923, and I took my rod and walked down to my old haunt by the Beehive bridge. I counted twelve black fish in the two meadows immediately below. There had not been a black fish in the Bourne—except in the starvation days—within the memory of man. I went straight back to the bridge and found what I was looking for. The tar-like dressing was thick upon the road, and it was ploughed up and furrowed by the engines which stop on it to water. The seams were gaping in the sun and the crude stuff was oozing in the gaps. The Beehive hill runs straight down to the bridge from the east and the steep Andover hill a couple of hundred yards away on the west ; both drain direct into the watershed of the Bourne.

They say that the tar-product now used is harmless, but the direct proof of the contrary was there before my eyes. The fish below the drainage outlet are turning black and carry the unmistakable brand of pollution.

The late Colonel Guy Baring, whose fish at Winchester were practically destroyed in a day by the first tarring of the roads, told me that he made some experiments in order to see for himself the process of destruction and the pace at which it worked. He put half a dozen trout into a tank of clear water and then

* This chapter was written in 1924.

dropped in a small bit of the tarred surface of the road outside. In three hours they were blind!

That, of course, was in the early days of ignorance and the authorities have lately done their best to get rid of the danger, but they have only partially succeeded. In the old days there was no tar on the Whitchurch road and there were no black fish in the river; it is draining into it to-day and there are a dozen of them in the two meadows immediately below the inlet.

The Bourne is a particularly hard case, for every shower of rain carries the surface washings from the two steep hills direct into the river. Even the intervening meadow at the foot of the Andover hill is useless as a filter-bed. The Bourne valley stands over a lake of running water (you know to an inch where you can strike it at any level); consequently the Andover hill drainage soaks right through the soil and into the water beneath and joins the river lower down.

If the Bourne is to be restored to her old glories, strong measures should be taken and taken quickly. First, the road authorities must be persuaded to withdraw the dressing from the roads for a good half-mile on either side of the village. These authorities, throughout the country, have been very sympathetic and have proved themselves capable of taking the large view of the question, and the appeal would probably not be made in vain. The objection is, of course, the dust along the few hundred yards of level road between the hills; but water has been the enemy of dust since the beginning of the world, and the water is running inexhaustible under the Beehive bridge. A primitive watering-cart would lay it at far less cost than they could lay the tar—and the Bourne might be saved.

Next, the river should be cleaned and the mud cleared off the spawning beds and gravel generally.

Next, the weed should be examined and if the shrimp is not there fresh supplies should be laid down. This would probably be useless if the tar were still coming down, for it is, no doubt, as fatal to the shrimp as to the fish, and to the duns as well. You might pick up a handful of weed at random anywhere in the Bourne in the old days and find enough shrimp kicking about in it to feed a two-pounder for a week.

Next, *when the river is clean*, the yellow-bellied trout should be cleared out lock, stock and barrel. They were introduced into the Test some five and twenty years ago and, like the American squirrel, they have ousted the original inhabitants which nature had put there and made fat and beautiful. They have not one redeeming feature. They are long and thin and poor and chicken-hearted, and defile the countryside like trippers and tin cans on Dartmoor. When they are gone the old Test fish must be put back. When the old cock Test trout reappears upon the spawning-beds there will be another chance for the Bourne.

Finally, when all is done, *the river should never again be overstocked*. Even from the point of view of sport, one fat, silver, hump-backed two-pounder is worth a hundred lean yellow cowards. The tragic history of that experiment is written in this book. If I can avert that calamity from any other river or save it from the slow death to which I tried to send this one, I shall feel that I have made some small atonement.

There never was a river that wanted less looking after than the Bourne before we overstocked it. The fish seemed actually to thrive upon short rations. There were long stretches of bare gravel without a patch of weeds in sight, where wooden artificial " hides " had actually been put down to give them shelter, and they seemed fatter and healthier and more beautiful there than anywhere. The cattle used to walk into the water and eat the weed, and it made no apparent difference to the food-supply. I have seen two-pounders and three-pounders swimming about the shallows with their back fins out of water and fairly bursting with health and defiance and high spirits. It was a wonder to us all how they managed it, for no one did a thing for them; nature did it all herself.

Exactly—nature did it alone, as she always will if you will not try to go one better. The secret of this river was that its watershed was fed by springs as clear and clean as crystal. In its three miles' run from the source it had no chance to pick up pollution. There were no mills to discharge their waste-products into those pure waters. The spawning-beds were spotless, the weed and the gravel veritable provision-stores, and the only worry in the lives of its inhabitants was the man on the bank. So they were born, and grew up and bred in the open, wild fish every one of them, and models to the Itchen or the Kennet or the Windrush or any other river in the British Isles. It was man that spoiled it all. If the Bourne is to be saved she must be given back to nature.

And so I say good-bye to her. The watercress beds above the viaduct have scarred her face and marred her beauty for ever. The pollard is there still, but the trees with the wild bees are gone. The black death is creeping through the chalk and covering her eyes with a film. Materialism has her in its grasp, and the road-hog must be served.

But somewhere, deep down, I have a dim hope that one night the fairy godmother will walk along the tarry road and stop on the bridge and listen, and send a message to me in the dark; and that when the mists begin to lift and the poplars to shiver and the cock-pheasants crow in the beech-woods, the little Bourne will wake and open her eyes and find in her bosom again the exiles that she had thought were gone for good—the silver trout, and the golden gravel, and the shrimp and the duns—and smell the dust of the road, and see the sun once more, and the red and white cows in the grass, and the yellow butter-cups in the meadow and the blue smoke of the cottages against the black elms of the Andover hill—and me, too, perhaps, kneeling beside her as of old and watching the little iron-blue, happy, laughing, come bobbing down to me under the trees below the Beehive bridge on the Whitchurch Road.

THE END